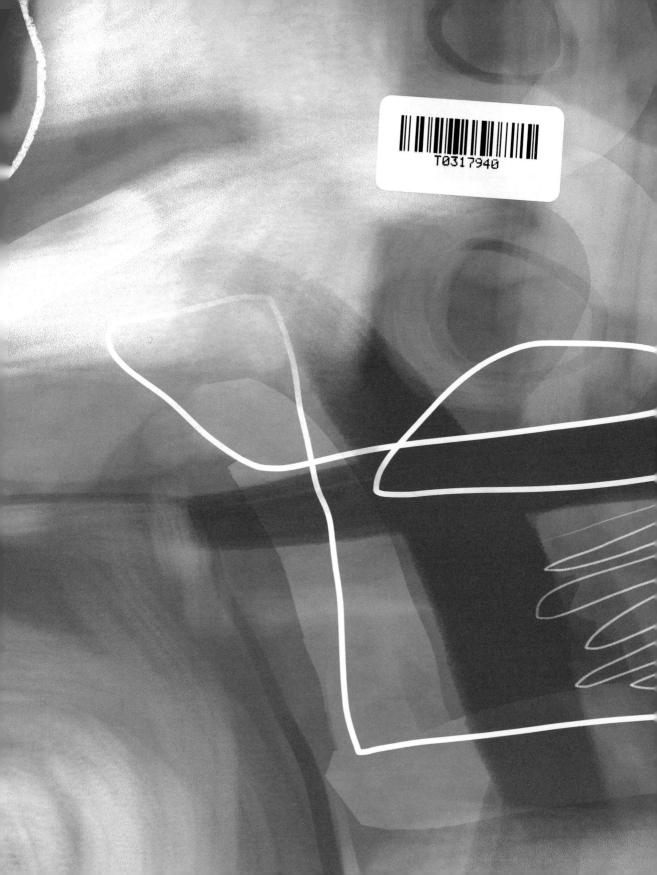

T0317940

HARLEM BREW SOUL

A Beer-Infused Soul Food Cookbook

CELESTE BEATTY

Founder of Harlem Brewing Company

ROCK
POINT

First published in 2024 by Rock Point, an imprint of The Quarto Group,
142 West 36th Street, 4th Floor, New York, NY 10018, USA
(212) 779-4972 www.Quarto.com

Rock Point titles are also available at discount for retail, wholesale, promotional and bulk purchase. For details, contact the Special Sales Manager by email at specialsales@quarto.com or by mail at The Quarto Group, Attn: Special Sales Manager, 100 Cummings Center Suite, 265D, Beverly, MA 01915, USA.

10 9 8 7 6 5 4 3 2 1

ISBN: 978-1-63106-851-5

Digital edition published in 2024
eISBN: 978-0-7603-7591-4

Library of Congress Control Number: 2024938648

Publisher: Rage Kindelsperger
Creative Director: Laura Drew
Senior Art Director: Marisa Kwek
Editorial Director: Erin Canning
Managing Editor: Cara Donaldson
Interior Design: Laura Klynstra
Back Cover and Interior Illustrations: Rahana Dariah
Photo Credit (p. 168): Patterson-Grant Reunion

HARLEM BREW SOUL is intended only for responsible adults of legal drinking age in the United States of America (21 years old or older). Please do NOT drink and drive. If you need transportation, use a designated driver or a taxi service. And please be careful when crossing the street after drinking.

HARLEM BREW SOUL does not advocate or encourage the abuse of alcoholic beverages. Please drink responsibly and in moderation. We do not, under any circumstances, accept responsibility for any damages that result to yourself or anyone else due to the consumption of alcoholic beverages or the use of this book and any materials located in it. We cannot take any responsibility for the effect these drinks may have on people. As such, we do not accept liability for any loss, damage, or inconvenience that occurs as a result of the use of this book or your reliance upon its content.

Dedicated to the vibrant spirit of Harlem, where culture, cuisine, and community converge. May this cookbook be a celebration of soulful flavors, bold brews, and the rich tapestry of traditions that inspire us to gather, savor, and create memories at the bar and around the table. Cheers to the fusion of two beloved worlds—beer and soul food—that fill our hearts and nourish our souls.

CONTENTS

BEEF, PORK & LAMB

BREWSERTS & BREAD

SAUCES, RUBS & BEERINADES

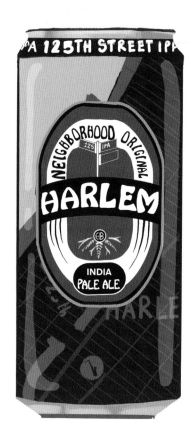

PREFACE

Harlem Brew Soul takes you from the streets of Harlem to the country roads of the Carolinas and back to the Festival of Drunkenness in ancient Kemet (Egypt) in 5000 BCE, where early beer culture was perfected using ancient ingredients. These brewing traditions helped fuel the building of the great pyramids and survived generations through oral cultural transmission, much like the poetic lines of Langston Hughes' "Harlem Sweeties."

Harlem holds a cultural importance to the African American that is akin to Jerusalem's significance and Bodh Gaya's reverence. This may explain why my family piled into the Buick station wagon with enough shoebox lunches (fried chicken and mac 'n' cheese) and lemonade for my mother, father, four siblings, and me to make the pilgrimage to Harlem, visiting family and stopping at the Apollo Theater, Studio Museum, Abyssinian Baptist Church, and Audubon Ballroom.

Cooking with beer is not new. It's been done since our ancestors made beer (hekt) with barley and emmer wheat in terra-cotta vessels. Beer hydrated, healed, and uplifted the spirits and, at times, provided sustenance when water sources were spoiled. It was drunk along the rails and rivers in the early 1800s in America, brewed and served up by the hands of Patsy Young, known as the Fugitive Brewer. Young was uncovered by Dr. Freddie Parker, professor emeritus of History at North Carolina Central University, in his book *Stealing a Little Freedom: Advertisements for Slave Runaways in North Carolina, 1791–1840*. We commemorated her contributions with our Fugitive Brewer Historic Ale, a collaboration with Rodg Little, brewer at Oak Park Brewing. The colonial style infuses North Carolina Loblolly pine needles (from farmer Earl Ijames in Johnston County), honey, molasses, and ginger. Beer recipes were passed down by her mother through demonstration and word of mouth, just like in ancient times in Africa. The essence of my culinary journey resonates deeply with the flavors, techniques, and ingredients passed down by my ancestors. Within these pages lies a tribute to their enduring resilience, boundless creativity, and cherished cultural heritage, as expressed through the soulful art of cooking.

Beer elevates flavor. Whether foraging in nature, your garden, or your fridge, there's plenty to pair or infuse with beer. This book reflects my years of dedication to uniting beer and soul food. Soul food, no matter where you experience it, will always take you back home. I always know where someone is from as soon as they tell me what they like to eat. I love croaker fish, and when I meet someone who also likes it, we pretty much know what town and state we're from. Food, like music, can place you at a time and "plate." Soul food is my center, my muse, because it holds the key to so much flavor and culture.

Harlem Brew Soul will guide you through the experience of learning to cook with beer to add layers of flavor from soup to nuts, literally. It's a collection of recipes and family stories about brew craft, community, and culture.

INTRODUCTION

Welcome to a culinary journey where soulful traditions meet the effervescence of craft beer—a collection inspired by heart, heritage, and hops. I'm thrilled to share these recipes, my cooking soundtrack for life, born from a passion for Southern soul food and the artistry of brewing.

As a brewer and founder of Harlem Brewing Company, my motivation stems from a desire to weave together this rich communal tapestry of African American cuisine with the diverse and dynamic world of craft beer. This book is a celebration of flavors, a symphony of tastes that pay homage to our roots while embracing the innovation found in a well-crafted brew.

My inspiring journey didn't just start in the brew house; it began at the family table,

where stories were shared, laughter echoed, and the aroma of soulful dishes mingled with Daddy's piano melodies, which filled the air like Fats Waller. The fusion of these beloved recipes with the robust essence of beer has been an enchanting journey—a tribute to the seamless fusion of tradition and ingenuity.

Join me on this culinary adventure, in which every recipe serves as a chapter in a story that unfolds on your taste buds. Let this cookbook be your compass through a world where heritage and creativity converge in delightful harmony.

So, grab a seat at the table, pour a glass of Harlem Brew, and let's relish the flavors that bind us together—a celebration of heritage, community, and the pure joy of sharing a meal with loved ones. Here's to the exciting journey ahead. Cheers!

HARLEM

I was born and braised in the Carolinas, and like many family members well before me, I eventually migrated up north to New York City—destination Harlem, the epicenter of all things Black culture—to join an amazing movement in Harlem's evolution. Some say a second Renaissance, long after the first Great Migration. Harlem was always making history. For me it was the most beautiful and elegant community in the world. Every stride I took on Harlem's streets was like stepping into a vibrant time machine, each step brimming with intention and history, from catching Cab Calloway's electrifying *Hi-De-Ho* at the Apollo

Theater to checking into the iconic Hotel Theresa.

Soul food was live from 125th Street and Fifth Avenue to Lenox Avenue and Frederick Douglass Boulevard and beyond, with deep roots from the Renaissance's Tillie's Chicken Shack to Crab Man Mike, just steps away from my own kitchen on 123rd Street. Down the street from the Apollo Theater was M&G's Fried Chicken, a family road-trip favorite. From east to west, north to south, and way uptown to Sugar Hill's Copeland's. Have you tried Famous Fish? Down-home cooked goodness was served up everywhere. The aromas of Sylvia's Restaurant's BBQ ribs converged with Spanish Harlem's Cuchifritos' pollo a la brasa, along with the Senegalese restaurants' thieboudienne on 116th Street, Jacob Restaurant, Amy Ruth's, Lenox Lounge, LaFamille, Gadabout (we go way back), Settepani, Sisters Cuisine, BLVD Bistro, Spoonbread, Manna's, Red Rooster, The Cecil, Billie's Black, Melba's, Field Trip, and so much more!

BREW

At some point, I met Garland Thompson, founder of Frank Silvera Writers' Workshop in Harlem. As an elder, he performed the Libation Ritual for the biannual National Black Theater Festival, pouring our Harlem Brew, accompanied by prayers, and invoking the ancestors, an offering to the gods and spirits. Could beer be the pathway to our past and future? A few weeks before the opening ceremony, I'd received a call from Garland: "Celeste, you got that Harlem brew ready? I'll be leaving Harlem at noon, headed to the Theater Fest." I was beyond honored.

I've always sensed a profound link between brewing beer and ancestral heritage and cultural identity. Beer holds a significant place within various spiritual traditions and cultural practices. It's remarkable to discover that the brewing customs I encountered in Africa have traversed generations through oral traditions and cultural exchanges among communities, such as the Ashanti and Yoruba tribes, even amid the challenging circumstances of the Middle Passage. These resilient traditions, encompassing brewing techniques, ingredients, and cultural rituals, were carried by our ancestors to the plantations, where they continued to thrive, evolve, and inspire. Despite the harsh conditions of slavery, they found ways to preserve and adapt these traditions, often through secret gatherings and ceremonies by incorporating local ingredients available on the plantations. Over time, these brewing traditions evolved and merged with other influences, creating unique forms of brewing that reflected the complex cultural heritage of enslaved people. Enslaved individuals were frequently tasked with various roles in the production process, including cultivating ingredients, such as grains or fruits, operating brewing equipment, and performing manual labor associated with brewing and fermentation. These recipes and techniques are well preserved through our oral history, whether speaking to someone in Harlem or anywhere in the South.

Growing up, I heard tales from my mom about our family's fermentation traditions—we had winemakers, brewers, and even a few moonshiners in the mix! But before delving into the fascinating history of African American brewing heritage, I must admit that beer didn't quite capture my interest. It often tasted watered down and bland to me. Yet, fueled by my passion for cooking with beer, I decided to tap into the world of brewing as a hobby. My brewing journey kicked off with a bang—or should I say a Kölsch! My first homemade beer, crafted from a five-gallon extract beer kit, was delightfully subtle and light; I affectionately labeled it HBK (Harlem Brew Kölsch). Determined to perfect this recipe, I focused all my energy on it before daring to tackle an all-grain Belgian witbier. Picture this: wheat, coriander, cumin—a flavor explosion waiting to happen—and I couldn't wait to get brewing.

SOUL

In the heart of Wilmington, North Carolina, in an area called the Crossroads, Sampson County, nestled among the sprawling fields and lush greenery, lay my grandparents' cherished farm. It wasn't just a place of work; it was a sanctuary, a haven where the soil whispered secrets of generations past, and the air hummed with the gentle melodies of nature's symphony. From dawn till dusk, they nourished the farm with unwavering dedication and boundless love. With weathered hands and a heart as vast as the horizon, my grandmother nurtured each plant as if it were her own child, coaxing life from the earth with a tenderness that knew no bounds.

As a child, I remember waking in the early morning light, the fields coming alive before my eyes like a bright rainbow: emerald lettuce leaves glistened with dew, plump tomatoes hung heavy on their vines, and rows of fragrant herbs danced in the breeze. It was a sight to behold, a testament to the magic that unfolds when human hands meet the fertile embrace of the land.

Summer afternoons were spent sipping sweet iced tea while wandering through the fields, barefoot and carefree, as we harvested, our baskets brimming with nature's treasures. We plucked ripe strawberries from their vines, their sweetness bursting on our tongues like sunshine in liquid form. We dug our fingers into the soft soil, unearthing potatoes and carrots as if finding buried treasure.

But it wasn't just the fruits and vegetables that captivated our senses; it was the sense of community that flourished amid the rows of crops, the bonds forged over shared meals and stories exchanged beneath the shade of the old pecan tree. Our table was a testament to the values that defined us: integrity, hard work, and an unwavering commitment to sustainability—it's no wonder why I joined the Future Farmers of America. In the evenings, as the sun dipped below the horizon and the sky blazed with hues of pink and gold, we gathered around the table to feast on the bounty of our collective labor.

But perhaps the most cherished moments were those spent in the kitchen, where my grandmother held court like a queen presiding over her kingdom. With flour-dusted hands and a bright twinkle in her eye, she guided us through the art of cooking, imparting wisdom passed down through generations with each flick of the wrist and dash of seasoning. It was here, in the heart of the kitchen, that the true magic happened, where simple ingredients transformed into culinary masterpieces that nourished both body and soul.

As I look back on those cherished memories, I am reminded of the profound impact my grandmother's farm-to-table traditions have had on my life. They taught me the value of hard work, the importance of sustainability, and the simple joy that comes from sharing a meal with those we love. Though my grandmother's farm may be but a memory now, its legacy lives on in every seed and rhizome planted, every meal shared, and every story told around the table. And as I carry forth her traditions into the world, I do so with a heart full of gratitude and a deep reverence for the land that sustains us all.

HIP-HOPS

What exactly is beer? It's a beverage made from fermented grains (malt, wheat, sorghum, etc.), hops, and yeast. It has long been the most social beverage in history and is the most popular alcoholic beverage consumed around the world. Here's a quick overview of the different styles of beer:

ABBEY: Beer that was once produced by monks in Belgium. Example: Dogfish Head Pêche de Tomme.

ALE (GOLDEN OR BLONDE): A crisp, refreshing, light-bodied beer that is gold in color. Example: Harlem Brewing Sugar Hill Golden Ale.

BARLEY WINE: A robust, malt-forward ale with high alcohol content and suitable for aging. Example: New Belgium Brewing Lips of Faith – Blackberry Barley Wine Ale.

BOCK: A strong, usually dark German lager that is slightly sweet. Example: Pilot Brewing Dunkles Bock.

BROWN ALE: A mild, malty brown beer associated with England and Scotland. Example: Two Locals Brewing Nubian Brown Ale.

DOPPELBOCK: German for "double bock," an extra-strong, dark version of bock beer. Example: Brooklyn Brewery Silver Anniversary Lager.

DUNKEL: German for "dark," any dark beer, usually a lager. Example: Aventinus Weizen Doppelbock.

FRAMBOISE: A Belgian-style lambic beer made with raspberries. Example: Montclair Brewery The Last Straw.

FRUIT: Beer made with fruit added as flavoring. Example: Full Circle Brewing Apricot Pie of the Tiger.

IMPERIAL STOUT: A very strong stout, 7 to 10 percent ABV. Example: Weathered Souls Brewing Rwanda French Press.

INDIA PALE ALE: A strong, bitter beer originally brewed in Britain for export to soldiers in India and now popular with beer enthusiasts. Example: Crown & Hops Inglewood Sun West Coast IPA.

KÖLSCH: A light, delicate, golden ale associated with Cologne, Germany. Example: Black Frog Brewery Aaliyah Raspberry Kölsch.

KRIEK: A Belgian lambic beer made with cherries. Example: Samuel Adams American Kriek.

LAGER (AMERICAN STYLE): A light-bodied beer with a refreshing taste and pale golden hues. Example: Rhythm Brewing Unfiltered Lager.

LAMBIC: A Belgian ale low in carbonation that is traditionally fermented only with wild yeast. Example: Cantillon Gueuze.

MAIBOCK: German for "May bock," a strong beer brewed in the fall and traditionally enjoyed in the spring, Example: Urban Growler Brewing Spring Fling!.

MÄRZEN: German for "March," a medium-to-strong malty beer brewed in March for consumption at fall celebrations, such as Oktoberfest. Example: Funkytown Brewery Homecoming.

MILD ALE: An amber, malty English-style ale with a lower alcohol content; a "session" beer. Example: Vine Street Brewing Street Lights.

OLD ALE: A British term for a medium-to-strong dark ale consumed in winter. Example: Wicked Weed Brewing Old Fashioned.

PALE ALE: A fruity, estery, milder version of an India pale ale. Example: Harlem Brewing 125th Street IPA; Atlantucky Brewing Ale Ale Cool J Double IPA.

PILSNER/PILSENER/PILS: A crisp, pale, hoppy lager. Example: Green Bench Brewing Postcard Pils.

PORTER: A malty, dark beer with a complex and flavorful character. Example: Métier Brewing Black Stripe Coconut Porter.

RAUCHBIER: A smoky-flavored lager developed in Germany that is made by wood-smoking the malt. Example: Sly Fox Brewing Smoked Helles Bock.

SAISON: A mildly sour, traditional Belgian summer ale flavored with spices or herbs. Example: Turner Häus Brewery Eliza.

STOUT: A richly malty or dry black beer. Example: Cajun Fire Brewing Big Chief; Harlem Brewing Queen Stout.

TRAPPIST: Beer made by Trappist monks. Example: Maredret Abbey Triplus.

UMQOMBOTHI: A South African traditional beer made from maize and sorghum malt, yeast, and water. Example: Tolokazi Sorghum Pilsner.

VIENNA: A reddish, sweet, malty lager originally made in Vienna, Austria. Example: Montclair Brewery MB Lager.

WEIZENBIER/WEISSBIER/HEFEWEIZEN/ BELGIAN WITBIER: A wheat beer. Example: Harlem Brewing Renaissance Wit.

WHAT'S ON TAP?

Throughout the recipes, you'll see Harlem Brews recommended in the ingredient lists, but feel free to use a similar-style beer. *Harlem Brew Soul* is all about encouraging improvisation while cooking.

LENOX LAGER

Lenox Lager embodies Harlem's heartbeat with golden hues, sweet, malty, herbal notes, and a light finish, paying homage to the pulsating rhythms of Lenox Avenue nightlife. ABV: 4.5%.

125TH STREET IPA

125th Street IPA has a refreshing, hoppy aroma that blends citrus and spice with a nutty-malt sweetness. Its hop-forward taste features layered earthy, fruity notes. Explore the Soul of Harlem's rich history and culture in every sip. ABV: 6%.

SUGAR HILL GOLDEN ALE

Sugar Hill Golden Ale is medium-bodied with a balanced malt sweetness, complemented by subtle citrus and hop notes. It's named after the Sugar Hill neighborhood, known for its cultural and economic prosperity during the Harlem Renaissance. ABV: 6%.

QUEEN STOUT

Queen Stout is a tribute to the powerful women in our lives, blending chocolate, coffee, and cinnamon. Named after our mother, Rachel Patterson Beatty Jackson, it celebrates sisters, mothers, grandmothers, aunts, and BFFs everywhere. ABV: 8%.

RENAISSANCE WIT

Renaissance Wit is a wheat beer lightly hopped with rich coriander, cumin, grains of paradise, orange peel, and natural orange flavors. It's a winner of Best Brews NYC's People's Choice Award. ABV: 5.1%.

OTHER HARLEM BREWS

Buck Leonard Lager, Route 64 Lager, Common Threads Pineapple & Hibiscus Pale Ale (a collab with Brixton Brewery), Grapricot Hefeweizen (a collab with Hippin' Hops Brewery)

SOME OF OUR FAVORITE BLACK-OWNED BREWERIES

- **Atlantucky Brewing** (atlantucky.com)
- **Montclair Brewery** (montclairbrewery.com)
- **Black Frog Brewery** (blackfrogbrewery.com)
- **Oak Park Brewing** (opbrewco.com)
- **Métier Brewing Company** (metierbrewing.com)
- **Full Circle Brewing** (fullcirclebrewing.com)
- **Green Bench Brewing** (greenbenchbrewing.com)
- **Two Locals Brewing** (twolocalsbrewing.com)
- **Turner Häus Brewery** (turnerhausbrew.com)
- **Vine Street Brewing Co.** (vinestbrewing.com)

Find more breweries at National Black Brewers Association (nb2a.org).

NOW WE'RE COOKIN' WITH BEER

To be honest, soul food is great with or without beer added to it. It's not so much the beer you're tasting, but what the beer brings out in food. Cooking with beer will enhance not only flavor but also tenderness. Adding beer is fun and easy. Just pour it on! Here are some general tips to follow when cooking with beer:

- Only cook with beer you enjoy drinking.
- Beer should lift and enhance food flavor and character, not drown it.
- Some easy ways to use beer while cooking are in sauces, marinades, and batters and for braising.
- Wheat beers are great with chicken and seafood.
- Ales, porters, and stouts are perfect for pork, beef, and lamb.
- Belgian ales work with hearty meats and game.
- Nut-brown ales pair well with stews and cheesy dishes.
- IPAs complement spicy foods and barbecue.

BEER SPEAK

While writing this book, I was feeling extra clever and created lots of beer-inspired portmanteaus that you'll come across throughout the book. Here are some you may see more than once:

- brewlicious = brew + delicious
- beerinade = beer + marinade
- beeraising = beer + braising
- broux = beer + roux
- brewsy = brew + boozy
- beernaigrette = beer + vinaigrette
- brilled = beer + grilled

. . . I think you get the gist!

GO-TO HERBS AND SPICES

- Allspice
- Basil
- Black pepper
- Cayenne pepper
- Chipotle
- Cilantro
- Cinnamon
- Coriander
- Cumin
- Garlic powder
- Ginger
- Himalayan salt
- Kosher salt
- Lemon pepper
- Onion powder
- Rosemary
- Sage
- Sylvia's Soulful Seasoned Salt
- Thyme

CRAFT BEER AND SOUL FOOD PAIRINGS

Pairing craft beer with soul food can create some delightful combinations, as both offer a wide range of flavors and textures. Complement the flavors in the beer to the flavors of the dish. For example, our Renaissance Wit beer is perfect as an ingredient for battering croaker fish but also for pairing with the dish. Here are a few general guidelines to consider:

1. **Match intensity.** Consider the intensity of flavors in both the beer and the dish. Rich, flavorful dishes, like fried chicken and barbecue ribs, can stand up well to bold, hoppy beers like IPAs, which can complement the savory and spicy elements of the food.

2. **Balance sweetness.** Soul food often incorporates sweet elements, like corn bread and candied yams. Pairing these dishes with beers that have malty sweetness, such as amber and brown ales, can create a harmonious balance of flavors.

3. **Contrast and refresh.** Sometimes, contrasting flavors can work well together.

For example, the bitterness of a stout or porter can cut through the richness of dishes like mac 'n' cheese and collard greens, providing a flavorful contrast.

4. **Consider carbonation.** The carbonation in beer can help reset the palate between bites, especially when enjoying dishes with rich sauces or fried foods.

5. **Experiment.** Don't be afraid to experiment with different beer styles and soul food dishes to find combinations that you enjoy. With the wide variety of craft beers available, there's no shortage of options to explore.

Ultimately, the best pairings will depend on personal preferences and the specific flavors and ingredients present in both the beer and the soul food dish. So, feel free to get creative and have fun with it!

Fried Chicken (Beer Fried Chicken and Waffles, page 108)
- Pale ale
- Wheat or Belgian witbier

Shrimp and Grits (Easy Cheesy Brewsy Shrimp and Grits, page 43)
- Saison
- India Pale Ale

Pulled Pork (Brewsy Pulled Pork, page 123)
- Stout
- Amber lager

Barbecue (Brilled Badass BBQ Ribs, page 126)
- India pale ale
- Porter

Salisbury Steak (Not My Dad's Salisbeery Steak, page 125)
- Amber ale
- Lager

Collard Greens (Beeraised Collard Greens in Queen Stout, page 73)
- Brown ale
- Porter

Corn Bread (Corn Beeread, page 150)
- Amber ale
- Hefeweizen

Macaroni and Cheese (Beer Smac 'n' Cheese, page 57)
- Pale lager
- Blonde ale

BEER COCKTALES

LOVE STORY

This book is a love story, not only about beer but also about discovering a history and tradition that I had no idea had any connection to my ancestors. Through experiences, travel to the motherland, and the living brewstories embedded almost verbatim in the memories of our families, friends, and neighbors throughout the United States, especially in the South, this collection of recipes covers everything you can imagine from appetizers to main courses.

My mother's table always welcomed friends; it was a gathering place to share their traditional soul food, dishes of Southern cuisine, from India, East and West Africa, and Central America. Before I could legally drink beer, I enjoyed my mom's infusions of tasty ginger beers and wine in homemade Southern and international dishes, along with a sip of Dad's brew. My mother would share her childhood stories about picking berries for Mrs. Annie Belle Smith's blackberry dumplings and family adventures discovering wild asparagus, okra, and polk salad along the roads. Years of family reunions taught us many great techniques: from Uncle Charlie's smoked turkeys and Aunt Bettie's pecan banana pudding to Aunt Pearl's fish fry and Cousin Vera's mac 'n' cheese.

Then we followed the path of relatives before us and headed north to the heart of Harlem, where Southern cuisine reunited full circle with Africa, the Caribbean, the Americas, and Europe and stimulated our taste buds. Travels to Africa and Central America introduced us to the many joys of grains of paradise (pepper) and cilantro, popular ingredients in some of our recipes.

HOPOLITAN

This cocktale is a unique blend of the vibrant flavors of a Cosmopolitan with some down-home charm. Sip and savor the harmonious union of citrusy hop notes, strawberries, and effervescent Lenox Lager, a refreshing twist that pays homage to both Cosmopolitan elegance and the soulful spirit of the South.

MAKES 1 DRINK

---

1 ounce (30 ml) Lenox Lager (or a similar beer)

1 ounce (30 ml) vodka

1 ounce (30 ml) orange liqueur

1 ounce (30 ml) fresh lime juice

½ ounce (15 ml) strawberry juice

Ice cubes

1 lime peel twist or fresh hops flower (if in season), for garnishing (optional)

1. Combine the beer, vodka, orange liqueur, and lime and strawberry juices in a cocktail shaker, then add ice.

2. Give it a Harlem shake and strain into a cocktail glass.

3. Garnish with the lime twist or hops flower (if using).

BENINI

A few years ago, I learned from a DNA test that my African ancestry included four countries: Senegal, Nigeria, Congo, and Benin. Beninese culture has many fresh fruits, including oranges, pineapples, mangoes, kiwis, and bananas, among others, which inspired this recipe.

MAKES 1 DRINK

2 ounces (60 ml) sparkling wine

1 ounce (30 ml) pineapple juice

1 ounce (30 ml) mango puree

2 ounces (60 ml) Renaissance Wit beer (or a similar beer)

1 pineapple slice, for garnishing

1. Pour the sparkling wine, pineapple juice, and mango puree into a chilled champagne flute.

2. Top off with the beer. Stir slowly to combine.

3. Garnish with the pineapple slice.

HARLEM PUNCH

Featured at the annual Harlem Week kickoff at Gracie Mansion with Mayor Michael Bloomberg in 2011, this punch is a perfect refreshment for any special occasion.

SERVES 20

---

3 cups (720 ml) water

2 cups (400 g) sugar

16 ounces (480 ml) cold pineapple juice

½ cup (120 ml) cold lemon juice

12 ounces (360 ml) cold orange juice

34 ounces (1 L) cold ginger ale

12 ounces (360 ml) cold Renaissance Wit (or a similar beer)

1. Add the water and sugar to a large pot over medium heat and stir until the sugar is dissolved to make a simple syrup. Remove from the burner and let cool.

2. Add the pineapple, lemon, and orange juices to a punch bowl with the cooled simple syrup. Stir well and chill in the refrigerator until ready to serve.

3. Before serving, add the ginger ale and beer. Serve cold.

NOTE: *Feel free to spike the punch with some rum or whiskey to taste.*

WOMOSA

A Womosa is a brewtiful, chic twist on the Mimosa, created with the modern woman in mind. This delightful libation combines the crispness of wheat beer with the bright and citrusy charm of a traditional Mimosa. To craft this refreshing elixir, simply mix equal parts of your preferred bubbly beer and chilled orange juice.

MAKES 1 DRINK

About 8 ounces (240 ml) orange juice

About 8 ounces (240 ml) Renaissance Wit (or a similar beer)

1 orange peel twist, for garnishing

1. Add the orange juice and beer to a pint or 16-ounce (480 ml) glass, then stir to combine.

2. Garnish with the orange peel twist.

BROMOSA BLITZ

This robust and flavorful cocktale marries the boldness of the 125th Street IPA with the zesty vibes of a Mimosa, creating a beverage that's as dynamic as it is satisfying. Raise your glass to the Bromosa Blitz—a drink that embodies beer-infused charm.

MAKES 1 DRINK

---

4 ounces (120 ml) orange juice

1 ounce (30 ml) whiskey (I like Uncle Nearest 1856)

2 ounces (60 ml) sparkling wine

6 ounces (180 ml) 125th Street IPA (or a similar beer)

1 orange slice, for garnishing

1. Add the orange juice, whiskey, and sparkling wine to a pint or 16-ounce (480 ml) glass, then stir to combine.

2. Top it off with the beer and stir again.

3. Garnish with the orange slice.

SUGARITA

A good beer margarita should always highlight the flavors of the beer, not hide it. This cocktale features Sugar Hill Golden Ale and is served in a glass with a honey and brown sugar–coated rim to complement its sweet malt and citrus notes.

MAKES 1 SERVING

Honey, for coating the rim

Coarse brown sugar, for coating the rim

2 ounces (60 ml) Sugar Hill Golden Ale (or a similar beer)

2 ounces (60 ml) tequila

1 ounce (30 ml) fresh lemon juice

½ ounce (15 ml) fresh lime juice

Crushed ice

1 lime slice, for garnishing

1. Chill a margarita glass.

2. Place the honey and brown sugar on separate small plates or saucers. Turn the chilled glass upside down and dip it first into the honey, twisting slowly to coat the rim, then coat the rim of the glass with brown sugar as you did with the honey.

3. Add the beer, tequila, and lemon and lime juices to a cocktail shaker. Give it a Harlem shake and strain into the prepared glass.

4. Add crushed ice and garnish with the lime slice.

BEBOP BLISS

Living and brewing in the birthplace of Thelonious Monk—Rocky Mount, North Carolina—is one of the coolest experiences. Immerse yourself in the rhythmic pulse of jazz with this Bebop Bliss, a libation inspired by the genius of Thelonious Monk and the improvisational spirit of bebop. Enjoy this cocktale "Straight, No Chaser" or "Round Midnight."

MAKES 1 DRINK

2 ounces (60 ml) whiskey (I like Uncle Nearest 1856)

1 ounce (30 ml) fresh lime juice

½ ounce (15 ml) honey

6 ounces (180 ml) 125th Street IPA (or a similar beer)

Ice cubes

1 candied lime slice (see Note), for garnishing

1. Add the whiskey, followed by the lime juice, honey, and beer, to a cocktail shaker.

2. Give it a Harlem shake and strain over ice into a margarita glass.

3. Garnish with the candied lime slice.

NOTE: *Here's how to make candied lime slices: Prepare a bowl with ice water. Using a mandoline or very sharp knife, slice 4 limes into ⅛-inch-thick (3 mm) slices, discarding the ends. Add 4 cups (960 ml) of water to a medium saucepan and bring to a boil over high heat. Once boiling, turn off the heat and add the lime slices. Stir gently until softened, about 1 minute. Drain the pan and transfer the lime slices to the prepared ice bath. To the same saucepan, add 1 cup (200 g) of sugar and 1 cup (240 ml) of water and bring to a boil over medium-high heat, stirring gently until the sugar dissolves. Reduce the heat to medium-low and add the lime slices. Let simmer for 45 minutes, or until the rinds are translucent. Place a wire cooling rack over a parchment-lined sheet pan. Transfer the cooked lime slices to the wire rack and let cool for at least 1 hour, or until they have hardened and are no longer sticky. Store in an airtight container.*

A TRAIN ELIXIR

This cocktale is inspired by the timeless rhythm of Duke Ellington's "Take the 'A' Train" and the soulful essence of Billy Strayhorn's composition. This enchanting libation features the rich and malty Sugar Hill Golden Ale, harmonizing with the smooth dance of brown sugar, the spicy kick of ginger, and the citrusy tang of lime. Let this elixir take your senses on a flavor-filled ride.

MAKES 1 DRINK

1 teaspoon brown sugar

6 ounces (180 ml) Sugar Hill Golden Ale (or a similar beer)

4 ounces (120 ml) ginger ale, lemon-lime soda, or lemonade

Ice cubes

Grated zest of 1 lime

Crushed ice

1 lemon slice, for garnishing

1. Add the brown sugar, beer, and ginger ale to a shaker with some ice cubes.

2. Give it a Harlem shake and strain into a Collins glass.

3. Add the lime zest, followed by the crushed ice, to the glass and stir.

4. Garnish with the lemon slice.

SUMMERTIME SHANDY

Inspired by "Summertime," the timeless tune sung by Louis Armstrong and Ella Fitzgerald, this cocktale captures the soulful sounds of a summertime jazz serenade with its melody of flavors that harmonize the warmth of whiskey, the sweetness of honey, and the crispness of the 125th Street IPA.

MAKES 1 DRINK

2 ounces (60 ml) whiskey (I like Uncle Nearest 1856)

1 ounce (30 ml) honey syrup

½ ounce (15 ml) fresh lemon juice

Ice cubes

6 ounces (180 ml) 125th Street IPA (or a similar beer)

1 lemon peel twist, candied lime slice (see Note on page 31), or fresh hops flower (if in season), for garnishing

1. Chill a coupe or wine glass.

2. Add the whiskey, honey syrup, and lemon juice to a cocktail shaker with ice.

3. Give it a Harlem shake until chilled, then strain into the chilled glass.

4. Top it off with the beer.

5. Garnish with the lemon peel twist, candied lime slice, or fresh hops flower.

SWING (DON'T MEAN A THING)

Sip into the rhythm of the '30s with this cocktale, a melodious blend inspired by the lively spirit of jazz. This lyrical libation combines the notes of fruit with the bright spirits of Sugar Hill Golden Ale and Renaissance Wit, creating a dynamic orchestra of flavors. Cheers to an extraordinary fusion of beer and fruity elegance that proves that swing truly doesn't mean a thing without the perfect sip!

MAKES 1 DRINK

Ice cubes

6 ounces (180 ml) Sugar Hill Golden Ale (or a similar beer)

6 ounces (180 ml) Renaissance Wit (or a similar beer)

1 ounce (30 ml) fruit liqueur of choice (such as raspberry, peach, or apple)

1 lemon or lime peel twist, for garnishing

1. Fill a pint or 16-ounce (480 ml) glass halfway with ice.

2. Add both beers, then stir gently.

3. Add the fruit liqueur and stir again.

4. Garnish with the citrus peel twist.

RENAISSANCE MULE

This refreshing, aromatic cocktale is a collaboration with mixologist Alexis Austin at Chez Messy in Harlem. It intermingles flavors perfectly for a summer sidewalk hang or a cozy night in with a good book.

MAKES 1 DRINK

1 ounce (30 ml) vodka (I like Tito's)

¾ ounce (22.5 ml) lychee juice

¼ ounce (7.5 ml) fresh-pressed ginger juice (see Note)

3 ounces (90 ml) Renaissance Wit (or a similar beer)

Ice cubes

1 lime slice, for garnishing

1. Add the vodka, lychee and ginger juices, and beer to a cocktail shaker with ice.

2. Give it a Harlem shake to blend the flavors.

3. Pour into a copper mug or your favorite glass. Garnish with the lime slice.

NOTE: *Though you can buy ginger juice, here's an easy way to make your own, especially for the small amount needed for this recipe: Peel a 3-inch (7.5 cm) piece of ginger root. Grate the ginger root with a medium grater over a bowl. Gather the grated ginger, place it in a paper towel or cheesecloth, and squeeze it over a bowl to collect the juice. Reserve the pulp for another use.*

HARLEM SHUFFLE

Let the Harlem Shuffle transport you back to the Harlem Renaissance, where artistic expression and vibrancy were in full swing. This sophisticated beer cocktale pays homage to the cultural richness of the time. Crafted with the bold and regal Queen Stout that is infused with the decadent essence of chocolate and coffee, this cocktale is a celebration of art, rhythm, and flavor. Here's to a sip of history!

MAKES 1 DRINK

1½ ounces (45 ml) bourbon

1 ounce (30 ml) coffee liqueur

½ ounce (15 ml) simple syrup

Dash of chocolate bitters

Ice cubes

12 ounces (360 ml) cold Queen Stout (or a similar beer)

Handful of fresh cherries

1. Add the bourbon, coffee liqueur, simple syrup, and chocolate bitters to a cocktail shaker. Give it a Harlem shake to blend the flavors.

2. Fill a highball or beer glass with ice cubes.

3. Pour the shaken mixture into the glass.

4. Slowly pour the beer into the glass.

5. Drop a handful of fresh cherries into the cocktail. Give the cocktail a gentle stir with a swizzle stick.

BREWFAST & BREWUNCH

BREWSTORY

On June 19, 2001, Harlem Brewing Company launched at the Studio Museum in Harlem on 125th Street and catered by Norma Darden, a former top model and founder of Spoonbread Catering. It was truly a community celebration. Just hours before, I'd taken the A train up to the Bronx to pick up a twenty-five-foot Penske truck. Hours later, my mother, her brother, my uncle Arthur (an NYC taxi driver) at the wheel of the rental truck, and I were sitting three across, bouncing on Route 9W on a Harlem Brew run upstate to Saratoga Springs, the truck swaying precariously, a dance of metal and momentum that left our hearts pounding in our chests—an adrenaline-fueled frenzy and exhilarating rush that came with the anticipation of the moment we'd been planning for: launch day!

We arrived at the brewery, just down the road from where Solomon Northup, author of Twelve Years a Slave and a locally renowned fiddle player, and his wife, a resort cook and kitchen manager, once lived. We loaded our chariot to the brim with pallets of ice-cold beer and headed back to Harlem. But as the miles stretched on, the once tranquil journey took on a hair-raising turn. Route 9W unfurled before us like a snake, its twists and turns threatening to test the mettle of even the most seasoned driver. The weight of our precious cargo added to the suspense, each curve a heart-stopping reminder of the delicate balance between control and utter chaos. The cases of beer teetered on the edge of oblivion, their contents clinking, sloshing, and swaying with each of Uncle Arthur's gravity-defying maneuvers.

The wind whipped around our heads, carrying the scent of freedom and adventure, while the distant city lights of Harlem beckoned like beacons in the night. And just when we thought we couldn't hold our breaths any longer, we emerged victorious, our truck triumphantly rolling into the vibrant streets of Harlem. We may have been battered and breathless, but we wore our adventure like a badge of honor, a testament to the wild spirit that drives us forward, through the twists and turns of life's grand journey. It was time for a cold one!

EASY CHEESY BREWSY SHRIMP AND GRITS

Our beer-marinated shrimp and cheesy grits recipe is an irresistible fusion of coastal freshness and down-home comfort. This culinary masterpiece captures the essence of the maize and shrimp I enjoyed so much when I visited Africa.

SERVES 6

CHEESY GRITS

24 ounces (720 ml) Renaissance Wit (or a similar beer)

1 cup (240 ml) coconut milk

2 cups (296 g) quick grits

1½ cups (168 g) shredded Gouda cheese

Dash of cayenne pepper

Salt

SHRIMP TOPPING

2 tablespoons canola oil

¼ cup (15 g) chopped scallion

1 clove garlic, finely chopped

⅛ teaspoon black pepper

Dash of ground cumin

1½ pounds (680 g) shrimp, peeled and deveined

Salt

2 tablespoons finely chopped fresh cilantro, for garnishing

1 teaspoon finely chopped fresh rosemary, for garnishing

1. **To make the cheesy grits:** In a large saucepan, combine the beer and coconut milk over medium heat. Bring to a boil, then mix in the grits. Reduce the heat and stir until thickened, 7 to 10 minutes.

2. Add the cheese to the pan and stir to incorporate. Season with the cayenne and salt. Remove the pan from the heat, cover, and keep warm while you make the topping.

3. **To make the shrimp topping:** In a large skillet, heat the oil over medium-low heat. Add the scallion, garlic, pepper, and cumin. Add the shrimp to the pan and cook and stir for 4 minutes, or until the shrimp turn pink and are opaque. Season with salt.

4. Divide the grits among bowls, top with the shrimp, and sprinkle with the chopped cilantro and rosemary.

BUTTERMILK WAFFLES WITH BEERAISED PEACHES IN SYRUP

It's Sunday morning: the aroma of waffles drifts through the kitchen and loved ones gather around the breakfast table. These waffles are a testament to the magic that can happen when simple ingredients come together. Golden and crisp on the outside, tender on the inside, and topped with beer-braised peaches, each bite is a journey back to cherished moments and the comfort of Grandma's home.

MAKES 8 WAFFLES

WAFFLES

3 large eggs

6 ounces (180 ml) Lenox Lager (or a similar beer)

1 cup (240 ml) buttermilk

½ cup (1 stick, or 115 g) butter, softened

2½ tablespoons vanilla extract

2½ cups (315 g) all-purpose flour

2½ teaspoons baking powder

1½ teaspoons baking soda

3 tablespoons brown sugar

½ teaspoon ground cinnamon

1½ teaspoons salt

Nonstick cooking spray

BEERAISED PEACHES IN SYRUP

1 tablespoon neutral oil

2 cups (310 g) sliced fresh or frozen (thawed) peaches

2 tablespoons granulated sugar

3 ounces (90 ml) Lenox Lager (or a similar beer)

1 teaspoon lemon juice

1 teaspoon vanilla extract

1. **To make the waffles:** In a large bowl, mix the eggs, beer, buttermilk, butter, and vanilla until thoroughly combined.

2. In a medium bowl, whisk together the flour, baking powder, baking soda, brown sugar, cinnamon, and salt.

3. Add the dry ingredients to the bowl with the wet ingredients and mix until just incorporated; do not overmix.

4. Spray a waffle iron with cooking spray and preheat.

5. Pour ½ cup (120 ml) of the batter into the waffle iron and cook for 3 to 4 minutes, until golden brown. Repeat with the remaining batter.

6. **To make the beeraised peaches in syrup:** In a medium saucepan, heat the oil over medium heat. Add the peaches, sugar, beer, lemon juice, and 2 tablespoons of water to the pan. Bring to a boil, then reduce the heat to medium-low and let simmer for 10 minutes, or until the peaches have slightly broken down and are syrupy.

7. Remove from the heat and stir in the vanilla. Let cool for a few minutes before serving with the waffles.

SALMON CAKES WITH SUPREME SAUCE

This dish brings together the flavors of family-style salmon cakes—a true taste of soul on your plate! Garnish with chopped parsley or chives for an added burst of color and freshness and enjoy with the supreme sauce for a flavor explosion.

MAKES 4 SALMON CAKES

SALMON CAKES

1 can (14.75 ounces, or 418 g) pink salmon

1 large egg

1 cup (125 g) all-purpose flour

2 slices bread, cubed

2 ounces (60 ml) 125th Street IPA (or a similar beer)

1 teaspoon finely chopped fresh cilantro

2 tablespoons finely chopped onion

Dash of paprika or cayenne pepper

Salt and black pepper

½ lemon, for squeezing

2 teaspoons vegetable oil

1 cup (150 g) medium cornmeal

Chopped fresh parsley or chives, for garnishing

1. **To make the salmon cakes:** Drain the liquid from the salmon and remove any bones. (You can also remove any skin, if desired.)

2. In a medium bowl, combine the salmon with the egg, flour, bread, beer, cilantro, and onion. Season with the paprika, salt and pepper, and a squeeze of lemon juice. Mix all the ingredients together until thoroughly combined.

3. In a large skillet, heat the oil over medium heat.

4. Divide the salmon mixture into 4 equal-size pieces and form into patties using your hands. Place the cornmeal in a shallow bowl and coat both sides of the patties in it.

5. Place the salmon patties in the hot skillet, working in batches if needed, and cook until browned on each side, 3 to 5 minutes.

SUPREME SAUCE

½ cup (120 ml) mayonnaise

2 tablespoons Dijon mustard

1 tablespoon hot sauce, or to taste

1 tablespoon honey

1 teaspoon apple cider vinegar

1 teaspoon Worcestershire sauce

½ teaspoon garlic powder

½ teaspoon onion powder

Salt and black pepper

6. **To make the supreme sauce:** In a medium bowl, stir the mayonnaise, Dijon mustard, hot sauce, honey, apple cider vinegar, Worcestershire sauce, and garlic and onion powders until well combined. Season with salt and pepper.

7. Garnish the salmon cakes with parsley or chives and serve with the supreme sauce.

THREE-CHEESE GRITS CASSEROLE

Gather 'round and pass the grits! This casserole is a journey through homegrown goodness and family tradition. In this hearty recipe—that's creamy, cheesy, and oh-so indulgent—these grits are a testament to the comfort and love that flows from our kitchen to your plate!

SERVES 6

1 cup (2 sticks, or 225 g) butter or margarine, divided

½ cup (75 g) chopped red bell pepper

½ cup (75 g) chopped green bell pepper

½ cup (75 g) chopped yellow bell pepper

¼ cup (15 g) chopped scallion

2 ounces (60 ml) Lenox Lager (or a similar beer)

3 cups (720 g) cooked grits

½ cup (120 ml) light cream

1 cup (115 g) shredded Cheddar cheese, plus 1 tablespoon for topping

1 cup (115 g) shredded pepper Jack cheese

1 cup (100 g) grated Parmesan cheese

1 teaspoon coarse salt, or to taste

1 teaspoon black pepper

1. Preheat the oven to 375°F (190°C).

2. In a large skillet, melt ¼ cup (½ stick, or 55 g) of the butter over medium heat. Add the chopped bell peppers and scallion and cook and stir until al dente, about 5 minutes. Transfer to a paper towel–lined plate to drain.

3. Butter a 2-quart (2 L) casserole dish with ¼ cup (½ stick, or 55 g) of the butter. Pour the beer into the buttered dish. Add a layer of one-third of the grits, then top with half of the bell pepper–scallion mixture, half of the cream, and half of the cheeses. Repeat this step with the grits, pepper-scallion mixture, cream, and cheeses and end with the remaining one-third of grits on top. Season with the salt and pepper.

4. Cut the remaining ½ cup (1 stick, or 115 g) butter into pieces and dot the top of the casserole with the pieces. Sprinkle with the remaining 1 tablespoon Cheddar.

5. Bake for 25 minutes, or until browned and crispy on top.

BREWSY BISCUITS AND SAUSAGE GRAVY

Savor a taste of tradition with these homemade biscuits and gravy. Crafted with love, this recipe is a celebration of our Aunt Mary's Ma Brown's Bakery, a very popular café and bakery that was in Durham, North Carolina. Her biscuits and baked goods were favorites locally as well as on military bases. She literally channeled Grandma Oni's soul food recipes, the same ones I have infused a hint of beer! Enjoy the warmth and richness of this family classic, in which biscuits and gravy take center stage in a sonata of taste and tradition.

SERVES 6 TO 8

BISCUITS

3 cups (375 g) all-purpose flour, plus more for dusting

1 tablespoon baking powder

2 tablespoons sugar

½ teaspoon kosher salt

½ cup (1 stick, or 115 g) cold unsalted butter, cut into small pieces

8 ounces (240 ml) Lenox Lager (or a similar beer)

SAUSAGE GRAVY

¼ cup (½ stick, or 55 g) unsalted butter

2 sausage patties, finely chopped

¼ cup (30 g) all-purpose flour

1 cup (240 ml) Lenox Lager (or a similar beer)

1 cup (240 ml) beef or vegetable broth

1. Preheat the oven to 425°F (220°C) and line a baking sheet with parchment paper.

2. **To make the biscuits:** In a medium bowl, combine the 3 cups (375 g) flour, baking powder, sugar, and kosher salt and mix to combine. Add the cold butter pieces to the bowl and work it into the flour mixture with your hands or a pastry cutter until it resembles pea-size crumbs. Pour in the beer and stir until a shaggy dough forms.

3. Place the dough on a lightly floured work surface and knead it for 1 minute. The dough should be smooth and no longer wet. Roll out the dough with a rolling pin until it is ¼ inch (6 mm) thick. Fold it in half. Using a 2-inch (5 cm) round cutter, cut out the biscuits and place on the prepared baking sheet, spaced apart. Fold and re-roll the remaining scraps, then cut out a few more biscuits.

4. Bake for 20 to 25 minutes, until the tops are golden and the biscuits have risen.

5. **Meanwhile, make the sausage gravy:** In a medium saucepan, melt the butter over medium heat until it is foamy. Add the sausage patties and cook until browned, while breaking them up into pieces, 3 to 5 minutes.

(continued)

1 tablespoon Worcestershire sauce

1 teaspoon Dijon mustard

Salt and black pepper

6. Whisk in the ¼ cup (30 g) flour until incorporated. Cook, whisking continually, for 2 to 3 minutes, until the roux is golden brown. Gradually pour in the beer while whisking constantly. Let simmer for a few minutes to cook off the alcohol and enhance the beer flavor.

7. Slowly pour in the broth, whisking to avoid lumps. Bring the mixture to a gentle simmer, stirring frequently for 2 minutes longer, or until thickened. Add the Worcestershire sauce and Dijon mustard and season with salt and pepper. Adjust the seasonings to your taste preferences. Continue simmering the gravy over low heat, stirring occasionally, until it reaches your desired thickness, 1 to 2 minutes longer. Remove from the heat. (If it is too thick, add more broth or beer to adjust the consistency.)

8. To serve, spoon the sausage gravy over the biscuits.

NOTE: *You can also enjoy this gravy with grits and mashed potatoes.*

CATFISH NUGGETS

These wheat beer–infused catfish nuggets are a tasty take on a traditional Southern favorite, inspired by the flavors of restaurateur Norma Darden of Miss Mamie's Spoonbread Too. This recipe's perfect balance of savory and aromatic ingredients entices the palate, combining the tender deliciousness of catfish with the subtle spices in the beer. This recipe was a featured appetizer for our brewery launch in 2001.

SERVES 4

8 ounces (240 ml) Renaissance Wit (or a similar beer)

1 teaspoon garlic powder

1 teaspoon onion powder

½ teaspoon paprika

½ teaspoon cayenne pepper, or to taste

Salt and black pepper

1 pound (454 g) catfish nuggets

1 cup (125 g) all-purpose flour

1 teaspoon baking soda

Canola oil, for frying

Favorite dipping or tartar sauce, for serving

1. In a large bowl, combine the beer, garlic and onion powders, paprika, and cayenne. Season with salt and pepper and mix well. Let sit for a few minutes to allow the flavors to combine.

2. Add the catfish nuggets to the bowl and thoroughly coat them in the beerinade. Cover the bowl and let marinate in the refrigerator for at least 30 minutes and up to 2 hours.

3. Place the flour and baking soda in a shallow bowl and season with salt and pepper.

4. In a large deep skillet, preheat the oil to 350°F (175°C).

5. Thoroughly coat each marinated catfish nugget by dredging it in the flour mixture.

6. Carefully lower the coated catfish nuggets into the hot oil and cook until crispy and golden brown, 3 to 4 minutes on each side, depending on the thickness of the nuggets. Transfer to a paper towel–lined plate to absorb excess oil.

7. Serve hot with your favorite dipping or tartar sauce.

STARTERS & SIDES

FAMILY REUNION (PART 1)

"My daddy was a poor man, but he made our lives rich," Mom stated about her father, Raymond Patterson.

Every July Fourth weekend, we gather for the Patterson-Grant Family Reunion, bringing together generations bound by the threads of love and tradition. The air fills with the enticing aromas of soul food, soul music, and catch-up conversations about family history, reminiscing about traditions and current events all stirring up dormant memories. The program includes live music, puppets, games, and the family talent show.

The weekend kicks off with a big fish fry featuring catfish, whiting, croakers, porgies, and the catch of the day. The side dishes include coleslaw, deviled eggs, baked beans, green salad, macaroni salad, mac 'n' cheese, sweet tea, punch, beer, wine, spirits, and so much more! Families gather around the tables, and then someone blesses the table full of food adorned with dishes passed down through the ages, an unspoken acknowledgment that this feast holds a special power. Aunt Pearl, with her fine, silver hair and a twinkle in her eye, presents the spread—a sensory masterpiece that will transport us all. Pass the collard greens!

BEER SMAC 'N' CHEESE

Baking mac 'n' cheese is an art, especially in our family. Everyone has their special technique. I can't tell you which aunt or cousin (by name) makes the best recipe, because I might cause a debate at the next family reunion, but I can tell you that I never turn down a good mac! I remember lining up for a surprise chance not only to meet Roberta Flack (yes, that Grammy-winning songstress) but also to taste her Arlington, North Carolina–style mac 'n' cheese at George Faison's Firehouse Theater reception in Harlem. It was smac 'n' cheese good!

SERVES 4 TO 6

---

1 pound (454 g) macaroni or shells

¼ cup (½ stick, or 55 g) butter

1 teaspoon all-purpose flour

½ teaspoon smoked cayenne pepper

1 large egg, beaten

6 tablespoons heavy cream

3 ounces (90 ml) Lenox Lager (or a similar beer)

1½ pounds (680 g) grated cheese of choice (I recommend Cheddar or Gouda)

4 slices cooked crispy bacon, chopped, for topping

1. Preheat the oven to 375°F (190°C).

2. Bring a large pot of water to boil, add the pasta, and cook for 4 minutes. Drain.

3. In a large skillet, melt the butter over medium-low heat. Once melted, whisk in the flour and cayenne pepper and continue whisking for 1 minute. Remove from the heat.

4. In a medium bowl, whisk together the egg, heavy cream, and beer.

5. Slowly whisk the cream mixture into the flour mixture, whisking constantly to avoid scrambling the egg.

6. Place the skillet back on the stove over medium-low heat. Switch to a wooden spoon and stir constantly until the mixture is thickened, creamy, and coats the back of the spoon, 3 to 5 minutes.

7. Add half of the cooked pasta to a 9 x 13-inch (23 x 33 cm) baking dish, then pour in half of the sauce and sprinkle with half of the grated cheese. Repeat with the remaining macaroni, sauce, and cheese.

8. Bake for 30 to 45 minutes, until the top is lightly browned and bubbly.

9. Top with the crispy bacon pieces.

TAILGATE BREWFFALO WINGS

Elevate your tailgate party with these hot buffalo-style wings that bring the perfect balance of heat and flavor. Infused with Lenox Lager and the fieriness of cayenne pepper, the robustness of garlic, and the boldness of black pepper, these wings are a game-day sensation. Get ready to impress your fellow fans with a dish that's a touchdown in every bite. Let's fire up the grill and make your tailgate legendary!

MAKES 12 TO 15 WINGS

3 pounds (1.4 kg) chicken wings (12 to 15 wings)

6 ounces (180 ml) Lenox Lager (or a similar beer)

1 teaspoon cayenne pepper

1 teaspoon garlic powder

1 teaspoon black pepper

2 tablespoons salt

Neutral oil, for frying

¼ cup (60 ml) red hot sauce

¼ cup (60 ml) soy sauce

½ cup (1 stick, or 115 g) butter, melted

Blue cheese dressing, for serving

1. Split the wings and add to a large bowl. Add the beer to the bowl, cover, and let marinate in the refrigerator for 1 to 2 hours. Drain the wings and allow to dry on paper towels.

2. In a small bowl, blend the cayenne, garlic powder, pepper, and salt. Sprinkle the spice rub over the dry wings.

3. Pour enough oil into a large, heavy-bottomed pot to cover the wings and allow them to spread out. Heat over medium-high heat.

4. Working in batches, deep-fry the wings for 15 minutes, or until browned and crispy. Transfer to a paper towel–lined baking sheet and keep warm with a foil tent while you fry the remaining wings.

5. In a large bowl, combine the hot sauce, soy sauce, and melted butter until thoroughly incorporated.

6. Add the fried wings to the hot sauce mixture and toss to evenly coat.

7. Serve with blue cheese dressing.

   NOTE: *Instead of frying the wings, you can bake them in an oven preheated to 400°F (205°C) for 40 minutes, or until browned and crispy, flipping halfway through the cooking time.*

HOPPY HOPPIN' JOHN

A staple at Grandma's table, Hoppin' John traditionally combines black-eyed peas, rice, and ham hocks to create a dish symbolizing good luck and prosperity. In this hopped-up recipe, we pour on the beer to add another layer of depth and complexity to the flavors, making it a deliciously unique experience that pays homage to African diasporic tradition while embracing creativity. Serve it as a side or a standalone dish.

SERVES 4

1 cup (165 g) dried black-eyed peas

4 slices bacon, chopped

1 medium onion, finely chopped

1 medium green bell pepper, diced

2 celery ribs, diced

3 cloves garlic, minced

1 cup (150 g) diced smoked ham

1 teaspoon dried thyme

1 teaspoon smoked paprika

Salt and black pepper

12 ounces (360 ml) 125th Street IPA (or a similar beer)

3 cups (720 ml) chicken broth

1 cup (190 g) long grain white rice

Chopped scallion, for garnishing

1. Put the black-eyed peas in a large stockpot, cover with cold water, and let soak overnight. (If you are short on time, you may cover the black-eyed peas with water in a large stockpot, bring to a boil over high heat, then turn off the heat and let sit for 1 hour.)

2. Drain and rinse the peas, then return to the pot and cover with fresh water. Bring to a boil, reduce the heat to medium-low, and let simmer for 45 to 60 minutes, until the peas are tender. Drain.

3. In a large Dutch oven or pot, cook the bacon over medium heat until crispy. Add the onion, bell pepper, celery, and garlic and cook and stir until tender, 5 to 7 minutes.

4. Add the ham, thyme, and paprika and season with salt and pepper. Cook for 2 minutes, stirring occasionally, to allow the flavors to blend.

5. Pour in the beer to deglaze the pot, scraping up any flavorful bits from the bottom. Add the broth and bring to a gentle simmer over medium-low heat.

6. Add the black-eyed peas and rice to the pot, stirring to combine. Cover the pot with the lid and let simmer over low heat until the rice is cooked and has absorbed the liquid, 20 to 25 minutes.

7. Once cooked, fluff the rice with a fork and season to taste. Garnish with chopped scallion.

SPICY COCONUT BEER-SPICED RICE

Unleash your taste buds with suds and savor the soulful tropical flavors in every bite of this coconut and beer–spiced rice! This recipe brings together the richness of coconut, the warmth of aromatic spices, and the subtle hoppy notes of lager, creating a dish that is both comforting and uniquely flavorful. Serve as a delightful side dish or add some beans for a more substantial meal.

SERVES 2 TO 4

---

1 cup (180 g) basmati rice

1 tablespoon coconut oil

1 medium onion, finely chopped

2 cloves garlic, minced

1 teaspoon ground turmeric

1 teaspoon ground cumin

½ teaspoon ground coriander

½ teaspoon chili powder, or to taste

1 can (13.5 ounces, or 400 ml) coconut milk

8 ounces (240 ml) Lenox Lager (or a similar beer)

Salt and black pepper

Chopped fresh cilantro, for garnishing

1. Rinse the basmati rice in a fine-mesh strainer under cold running water until the water runs clear. Soak the rice in a bowl of fresh water for 15 to 20 minutes. Drain.

2. In a large saucepan, heat the coconut oil over medium heat. Cook and stir the onion until softened and translucent, 3 to 5 minutes. Add the garlic and cook until fragrant, about 1 minute.

3. Add the turmeric, cumin, coriander, and chili powder, stirring constantly for 30 seconds, allowing the spices to release their flavors. Be careful not to burn them.

4. Pour in the coconut milk and beer and stir well to combine. Bring the mixture to a gentle simmer over medium heat.

5. Add the rice to the pan and season with salt and pepper. Cover the pan with the lid and reduce the heat to low. Let the rice cook for 15 to 20 minutes, until tender and the liquid is absorbed. Turn off the heat, leave covered, and let sit for 5 minutes.

6. Fluff the rice with a fork, then serve garnished with chopped cilantro.

CHEF K'S JAZZY WINGS

When the Beer Chef does wings . . . Infused with garlic, onion powder, paprika, and a touch of adobo spice, these wings will take you to a whole new level with the addition of Sugar Hill Golden Ale beerinade. The result is a tantalizing fusion of spicy, zesty goodness. Fire up the grill and get ready to lick your fingers while savoring every delicious bite of these soul food–inspired, jazzy, grilled wings.

MAKES 8 TO 10 WINGS

---

4 cloves garlic, minced

1 teaspoon onion powder

1 tablespoon paprika

1 teaspoon salt

1 tablespoon adobo seasoning

2 pounds (907 g) chicken wings

8 ounces (240 ml) Sugar Hill Golden Ale (or a similar beer), plus more for basting

Bar-Beer-Que Sauce (page 162) or favorite dipping sauce, for serving

1. Make the spice rub by combining the garlic, onion powder, paprika, salt, and adobo seasoning in a small bowl.

2. Pat the chicken wings dry and generously coat them with the spice rub. Place the seasoned wings in a resealable plastic bag or shallow dish, then pour the beer over them. Let marinate in the refrigerator for at least 2 hours, or overnight.

3. Preheat a grill to medium-high heat. Remove the wings from the beerinade, allowing any excess liquid to drain off. Grill the wings for 15 to 20 minutes, turning occasionally, until they are cooked through and have a nice char. For an extra layer of flavor, baste the wings with additional beer during grilling.

4. Serve hot with bar-beer-que or your favorite dipping sauce.

NOTE: *The wings can also be baked or cooked on the stovetop in a cast-iron skillet: If baking in the oven, preheat it to 400°F (205°C). Line two baking sheets with aluminum foil and fit them with wire racks. Remove the wings from the beerinade and pat dry, then arrange them in a single layer on the wire racks, making sure they do not touch each other. Bake for 40 to 50 minutes, until the skin is browned and crispy and the internal temperature reaches 165°F (74°C). If cooking on a stovetop, preheat a 12-inch (30 cm) cast-iron skillet that has a lid over medium-high heat for 4 to 5 minutes. Add a thin layer of avocado oil, about 1 tablespoon, and heat for 1 minute longer. Remove the wings from the beerinade and pat dry, then add a single layer of wings to the pan, working in batches so as not to overcrowd the pan. Let the wings fry for 4 to 5 minutes, until golden brown. Flip over and fry for another 4 to 5 minutes. Cover the skillet with the lid, reduce the heat to medium-low, and cook until the wings' internal temperature reaches 165°F (74°C), 10 to 15 minutes, flipping them halfway through the cooking time. Remove the lid, increase the heat to medium-high, and cook for 1 minute longer per side, or until crispy.*

HARLEM-STYLE BEER NUTS

These beer nuts combine the earthy crunch of pecans, walnuts, almonds, and peanuts with the golden warmth of ale, creating a snack that's both satisfying and irresistible. Infused with fresh thyme, rosemary, pepper, sea salt, and a hint of nutmeg, these beer nuts are the perfect companion for gatherings or a cozy night in.

SERVES 4 TO 6

12 ounces (360 ml) Sugar Hill Golden Ale (or a similar beer)

1 cup (100 g) pecans

1 cup (100 g) walnuts

1 cup (140 g) almonds

1 cup (150 g) peanuts

2 tablespoons finely chopped fresh thyme leaves

1 tablespoon finely chopped fresh rosemary

1 teaspoon black pepper

1 teaspoon sea salt, or to taste

½ teaspoon freshly grated nutmeg

2 tablespoons unsalted butter, melted

1. Preheat the oven to 350°F (175°C). Line a baking sheet with parchment paper.

2. In a medium saucepan, heat the beer over medium heat until simmering, then let simmer for 5 to 10 minutes to reduce slightly. Remove from the heat and let cool.

3. In a large bowl, combine the pecans, walnuts, almonds, and peanuts. Pour the warm beer over the nuts and let soak for 15 to 20 minutes to absorb the beer flavor.

4. In a small bowl, combine the thyme, rosemary, pepper, salt, and nutmeg and blend well. Sprinkle the spice blend over the nuts.

5. Drizzle the melted butter over the nuts and toss them until well coated with the beer, butter, and spices. Evenly spread the nuts on the prepared baking sheet in a single layer.

6. Bake for 15 to 20 minutes, until the nuts are golden and fragrant. Stir them halfway through the cooking time to ensure even roasting.

7. Let the nuts cool completely before serving. Once cool, store in an airtight container in the refrigerator for up to 2 weeks.

CHEESY BREWSY DIP

We love to share this dish at tailgates, Monday Night Football watch parties, or just hanging out with family and friends. Serve it with crackers, chunks of bread, or soft pretzels for dippin' while you're sippin'.

SERVES 4 TO 6

---

2 tablespoons unsalted butter

½ cup (65 g) all-purpose flour

1 teaspoon smoked cayenne pepper

½ teaspoon mustard powder

1 tablespoon onion powder

1 cup (240 ml) milk

8 ounces (240 ml) Buck Leonard Lager (or a similar beer)

½ cup (55 g) shredded Cheddar cheese

½ cup (55 g) shredded Gouda cheese

2 tablespoons chopped fresh cilantro, parsley, or chives, for garnishing

Bacon bits, for garnishing

Crackers, bread, and/or soft pretzels, for serving

1. In a medium skillet, melt the butter over medium heat. Add the flour and whisk until smooth.

2. Add the cayenne, mustard, onion powder, and milk and whisk to combine well.

3. Add the beer and shredded cheeses and whisk until smooth and melted, 3 to 4 minutes.

4. Garnish with the chopped cilantro, parsley, or chives and bacon bits and serve with crackers, bread, and/or soft pretzels.

SPICY BEER-BATTERED FRIED GREEN TOMATOES

This recipe gives classic fried green tomatoes a kick of spice that perfectly complements the beer-infused batter. The marriage of tangy green tomatoes, a crispy coating, and a touch of heat creates a harmonious blend of flavors for the perfect appetizer or side dish.

SERVES 4 TO 6

1 cup (125 g) all-purpose flour

1 teaspoon baking powder

1 teaspoon cayenne pepper, or to taste

1 teaspoon garlic powder

1 teaspoon onion powder

Salt and black pepper

8 ounces (240 ml) Sugar Hill Golden Ale (or a similar beer)

Vegetable oil, for frying

4 large green tomatoes, sliced into ¼-inch-thick (6 mm) rounds

Favorite dipping sauce, for serving

1. In a medium bowl, whisk together the flour, baking powder, cayenne, and garlic and onion powders. Season with salt and pepper.

2. Slowly pour in the beer, whisking continuously to create a smooth batter. Let rest for 10 minutes.

3. In a large deep skillet, heat enough vegetable oil over medium-high heat for frying to 350°F (175°F), about 1 inch (2.5 cm) deep. (The oil is hot enough when you add a little batter, and it bubbles and floats to the surface immediately.)

4. Dip each green tomato slice into the beer batter, ensuring a thorough coating. Carefully place the battered green tomato slices into the hot oil, frying in batches to avoid overcrowding. Fry until golden brown on both sides, 2 to 3 minutes per side. Use a slotted spoon to transfer the fried green tomatoes to a paper towel–lined plate to absorb excess oil.

5. Sprinkle with an extra dash of salt and cayenne pepper for an added burst of flavor.

6. Serve hot with your favorite dipping sauce.

BEER-BATTERED SOUTHERN FRIED OKRA

This recipe elevates a classic family favorite, infusing it with a crisp and flavorful Lenox Lager batter. The combination of the crunchy exterior and the tender, succulent interior of the fried okra, enhanced by a perfect balance of salt and pepper, creates a dish that's both comforting and exciting.

SERVES 6

1 cup (125 g) all-purpose flour

1 teaspoon baking powder

1 teaspoon salt, plus more to taste

½ teaspoon black pepper, plus more to taste

8 ounces (240 ml) Lenox Lager (or a similar beer)

Vegetable oil, for frying

1 pound (454 g) fresh okra, trimmed and sliced into ½-inch-thick (13 mm) rounds

1. In a medium bowl, combine the flour, baking powder, salt, and black pepper and mix well. Slowly whisk in the beer until a smooth, lump-free batter forms. Let rest for 10 minutes.

2. In a large deep skillet, heat enough vegetable oil over medium-high heat for frying to 350°F (175°F), about 1 inch (2.5 cm) deep. (The oil is hot enough when you add a little batter, and it bubbles and floats to the surface immediately.)

3. Dip each okra piece into the beer batter, ensuring a thorough coating.

4. Gently place the battered okra into the hot oil, frying in batches to avoid overcrowding. Fry until golden brown, 3 to 4 minutes per batch. Use a slotted spoon to transfer the fried okra to a paper towel–lined plate to absorb excess oil.

5. Season with a sprinkle of salt and pepper and serve hot.

BEERED BEANS AND RICE

Billy Strayhorn wrote the lyrics and music to the jazz standard "Take the 'A' Train," which became a signature composition of Duke Ellington and his band. But did you know that another hit was his red beans and rice made with beer?

SERVES 6 TO 8

1 pound (454 g) dried red kidney beans

2 tablespoons neutral oil

1 package (12 ounces, or 340 g) smoked andouille sausage, thinly sliced

¼ cup (35 g) diced green bell pepper

¼ cup (30 g) diced onion

½ cup (50 g) diced celery

2 tablespoons unsalted butter

2 tablespoons (18 g) minced garlic (about 8 cloves)

1 teaspoon dried rosemary

1 teaspoon dried thyme

1 tablespoon smoked paprika

1 tablespoon onion powder

4 bay leaves

3 cups (720 ml) 125th Street IPA (or a similar beer)

24 ounces (720 ml) chicken broth

Salt and black pepper

Cooked rice, for serving

2 tablespoons finely chopped fresh cilantro, for garnishing

1. Soak the beans in water overnight, or in hot just-boiled water, covered, for 45 minutes.

2. In a Dutch oven, heat the oil over medium heat. Add the sausage slices and cook and stir until browned, about 5 minutes. Remove from the pot, maintaining the stove's heat.

3. Add the bell pepper, onion, and celery to the same pot with any of the sausage drippings and stir. Add the butter, garlic, rosemary, thyme, paprika, onion powder, and bay leaves and stir to coat. Cook, stirring occasionally, for 5 to 7 minutes, until the onion is tender and translucent.

4. Drain the beans and add them to the pot. Stir in the beer and broth and bring to a boil over medium-high heat. Reduce the heat to medium-low, cover with the lid, and let cook for 1 hour, stirring as needed. Season with salt and black pepper and remove and discard the bay leaves.

5. Serve over rice and garnish with the chopped cilantro.

BEERAISED COLLARD GREENS IN QUEEN STOUT

Collard greens are the official vegetable of Southern cuisine! And these beer-braised collard greens bring together the hearty goodness of collard greens, slow-cooked to perfection in a rich and flavorful stout-beer broth. This family favorite embodies the heart and soul of Southern comfort cooking—with a touch of brewspiration!

SERVES 4

2 tablespoons olive oil

1 large onion, finely chopped

3 cloves garlic, minced

1 cup (240 ml) vegetable broth

8 ounces (240 ml) Queen Stout (or a similar beer)

1 tablespoon apple cider vinegar, plus more to taste

2 teaspoons brown sugar

1 teaspoon smoked paprika

½ teaspoon red pepper flakes

Salt and black pepper

2 bunches collard greens, large stems removed and leaves roughly chopped

1. In a large skillet, heat the olive oil over medium heat. Add the onion and garlic and cook and stir until the onion is translucent, 3 to 5 minutes.

2. Add the broth, beer, apple cider vinegar, brown sugar, paprika, and red pepper flakes and season with salt and pepper. Mix well and let simmer for 5 minutes.

3. Add the chopped collard greens and stir well to thoroughly coat the greens with the liquid.

4. Reduce the heat to low and cover with the lid. Let the collard greens simmer and braise for 30 to 40 minutes, until tender. Add more salt and/or pepper if necessary.

5. Dash a bit of vinegar on the collards just before serving to enhance the flavor.

SCALLOPED POTATOES IN A WHEAT BEER SAUCE

This traditional comfort food combines the hearty goodness of thinly sliced potatoes with the smooth, malty notes of a wheat beer–infused sauce. Each layer is a masterpiece of creamy indulgence, making this dish a perfect companion to many entrées.

SERVES 6 TO 8

Nonstick cooking spray

4 tablespoons unsalted butter, divided

2 cloves garlic, minced

¼ cup (30 g) all-purpose flour

8 ounces (240 ml) Renaissance Wit (or a similar beer)

2 cups (480 ml) whole milk

1 teaspoon Dijon mustard

Salt and black pepper

4 large russet potatoes, peeled and sliced into ⅛-inch-thick (3 mm) rounds

2 cups (230 g) shredded Gruyère or Swiss cheese

Chopped fresh chives or parsley, for garnishing (optional)

1. Preheat the oven to 375°F (190°C). Grease a 9 x 13-inch (23 x 33 cm) baking dish with cooking spray.

2. In a saucepan, melt 3 tablespoons of the butter over medium heat. Add the garlic and cook and stir until fragrant, about 1 minute. Whisk in the flour until smooth and incorporated. Cook, whisking constantly, for 2 to 3 minutes, until the roux achieves a light golden color.

3. Whisk in the beer, followed by the milk. Continue whisking until the sauce thickens, 2 to 3 minutes. Whisk in the Dijon mustard and season with salt and pepper. Remove from the heat.

4. In the prepared baking dish, layer half of the sliced potatoes, followed by half of the shredded cheese.

5. Pour half of the beer sauce evenly over the potato and cheese layers. Repeat with the remaining potatoes and cheese, pouring the remaining beer sauce evenly over the top.

6. Cut the remaining 1 tablespoon butter into small pieces and dot the top layer.

7. Cover the baking dish with aluminum foil and bake for 45 minutes. Uncover and bake for an additional 15 to 20 minutes, until the top is golden brown and the potatoes are tender.

8. Let rest for a few minutes before serving. Garnish with the chopped chives or parsley (if using).

HIP-HOP COLESLAW

Hip-hop coleslaw is a fresh take on traditional coleslaw, with freestyle flavors that are sure to make your palate dance. This recipe brings together crisp cabbage, crunchy celery, and a blend of horseradish, mustard, cayenne pepper, and 125th Street IPA, all harmonized with the smooth vibes of mayonnaise and apple cider vinegar.

SERVES 6 TO 8

1 head green cabbage (1½ pounds, or 680 g), shredded or thinly sliced

1 large carrot, shredded or thinly sliced

1 rib celery, shredded or thinly sliced

1 cup (240 ml) mayonnaise

2 tablespoons prepared horseradish

1 teaspoon mustard powder

¼ teaspoon sugar

¼ teaspoon salt

¼ teaspoon cayenne pepper

2 tablespoons apple cider vinegar

1 ounce (30 ml) 125th Street IPA (or a similar beer)

1. Place the cabbage, carrot, and celery in a large bowl.

2. Add the mayonnaise, horseradish, mustard, sugar, salt, cayenne, vinegar, and beer. Season to taste.

3. Toss well to evenly combine and coat the ingredients. Cover and refrigerate for at least 1 hour before serving.

SOUTHERN BREWSHI ROLL

My mom told me that when she was growing up, if a woman wanted to be considered good marriage material, she had to cook good rice. She said that "if your rice didn't fall to the side," you were out of luck. Rice should stand on its own and not be sticky. Unless it's sushi rice.

SERVES 4

¼ teaspoon salt, plus more to taste

1 cup (205 g) sushi rice, rinsed and drained

1 sweet potato, peeled and cut into ¼-inch-thick (6 mm) strips

2 teaspoons vegetable oil

1 teaspoon honey

4 large collard green leaves

1 tablespoon coconut oil

12 medium-size raw shrimp, peeled and deveined

1 clove garlic, minced

3 ounces (90 ml) Renaissance Wit (or a similar beer)

1 cucumber, cut into ¼-inch-thick (6 mm) sticks

1 avocado, peeled, pitted, and sliced

1 tablespoon smoked paprika

Salt and black pepper

Soy sauce, for serving (optional)

Pickled ginger or seaweed, for serving (optional)

1. Preheat the oven to 400°F (205°C).

2. Combine the salt with 2 cups (480 ml) of water in a small pot and bring to a boil. Add the rice, cover with the lid, reduce the heat to low, and cook until all the water is absorbed and the rice is tender, 15 to 20 minutes.

3. Meanwhile, place the sweet potato strips on a baking sheet, toss with the vegetable oil, and season with a pinch each of salt and pepper. Roast until tender and browned in places, 10 to 12 minutes. Let cool, then brush with honey.

4. Bring a large pot of water to a boil. While the water is coming to a boil, prepare a large bowl with ice water. Add the collard green leaves to the boiling water and blanch until bright green, about 2 minutes. Remove from the boiling water and transfer to the prepared ice bath.

5. In a medium skillet, heat the coconut oil over medium heat. Add the shrimp, garlic, and beer and let simmer for 4 minutes, or until the shrimp are pink and opaque. Remove from the pan and, when cool enough to handle, cut the shrimp into small pieces. Discard the beer.

(continued)

6. Remove the collard greens from the ice bath and dry on paper towels. Spread a leaf on a work surface, stem side up (the stem forms a large ridge down the back of the leaf). Using a sharp, non-serrated knife, cut as much of the stem off as you can without cutting through the leaf itself (i.e., hold your knife perpendicular to the leaf and gently slice away as much of the ridge of stem as possible; this will make the leaf more pleasant to eat and easier to roll). Slice off the entire stem at the base of the leaf and flip the leaf over. Repeat with the remaining collard green leaves.

7. With damp fingers, spread a ½-inch (13 mm) layer of rice, leaving a 1-inch (2.5 cm) edge at the top of the leaf for sealing the roll. Lay one-quarter of the sweet potato, cucumber, avocado, and shrimp in a thin layer one-third of the way down the rice and sprinkle with some of the paprika. To roll, fold the bottom of the leaf up over the ingredients, then fold in the sides. Use your fingers to hold the ingredients tight and roll away from you until the roll is almost closed. You can finish rolling as is, but I like to add a small dab of water to the last little bit of leaf so that it sticks and holds itself closed a little better. Repeat with the remaining collard leaves, fillings, and paprika.

8. Slice each roll into six 1-inch (2.5 cm) slices and, if you like, serve with soy sauce and pickled ginger or seaweed.

SOUPS & STEWS

FAMILY REUNION (PART 2)

The first bite is a revelation. The crispy crunch of fried chicken echoes through time, triggering a deep rush of childhood memories that had been forgotten. Laughter and chatter melt away as each family member succumbs to the enchantment of flavors. The collard greens, slow-cooked to perfection, whisper stories of Sunday dinners and cherished secrets.

Uncle Aaron and Uncle Charlie and sons serve up their legendary BBQ pulled pork and smoked turkeys. All the aunts and daughters share their signature mac 'n' cheeses, a creamy concoction that tastes like hugs and warmth. As the velvety richness dances on the taste buds, forgotten afternoons spent in Grandma's kitchen come flooding back. The corn bread, golden and crumbly, carries the echoes of childhood giggles and tales spun around the television. It's a journey waay back in time, with every bite unlocking another chapter of our family's shared history.

In the midst of this sensory extravaganza, The O'Jays' "Family Reunion," a time-honored tune, plays softly in the background—the soulful melodies of Motown. Suddenly, the room transforms into a dance floor, and the older generation twirls the younger ones around, passing down not only recipes but also the rhythm of their joy. As the feast reaches its crescendo, it is time to break out the banana pudding, sweet potato pie, and pound cakes, their fragrance a gateway to the past. Each forkful becomes a portal to forgotten birthdays, holiday gatherings, and the comforting embrace of a family that has weathered storms together.

The Patterson-Grant family's soul food sensory experience isn't just a meal; it is a reunion with the essence of our shared identity. As the last crumbs disappear, we leave the table with our hearts full, carrying the taste of nostalgia and the warmth of a love that spans generations.

BREWLICIOUS CHICKEN BARLEY SOUP

This soul-warming creation brings together tender chicken, hearty barley, and Sugar Hill Golden Ale, resulting in a comforting bowl that's simply brewlicious.

SERVES 6 TO 8

1½ tablespoons neutral oil

1½ tablespoons butter

2 cups (140 g) sliced mushrooms

½ cup (55 g) chopped onion

2 ribs celery, chopped

3 medium carrots, peeled and chopped

3 cloves garlic, minced

¼ cup (30 g) all-purpose flour

8 cups (1.9 L) water or chicken broth

2 cups (400 g) pearl barley

1 tablespoon salt, plus more to taste

1½ tablespoons black pepper, plus more to taste

½ teaspoon finely chopped fresh rosemary

6 ounces (180 ml) Sugar Hill Golden Ale (or a similar beer)

1 cup (240 ml) heavy cream

3 cups (585 g) cubed cooked chicken, juices reserved

¼ cup (10 g) finely chopped fresh cilantro, for garnishing

1. In a large pot, heat the oil and butter over medium heat. Add the mushrooms, onion, celery, carrots, and garlic and cook until tender, 4 to 5 minutes, stirring occasionally. Add the flour, stirring continually and coating the vegetables.

2. Add the water or broth, along with the barley, salt, pepper, and rosemary and bring to a boil over medium-high heat. Reduce the heat to medium-low and cook until the barley is tender, about 30 minutes.

3. Add the beer, cream, and chicken and its juices and let simmer for an additional 15 minutes on medium-low. Season with salt and pepper.

4. Ladle into bowls and serve hot topped with chopped cilantro.

   NOTE: *Enjoy with a slice of corn bread or Corn Beeread (page 150).*

SEAFOOD GUMBREW

Each spoonful of this gumbo is a celebration of Southern culinary tradition with a contemporary twist. For several years, I attended the gumbo cook-off at Dr. George Preston's Museum of Art and Origins (MOAO) in Harlem, which features a breathtaking collection of African art.

SERVES 6

½ cup (120 ml) canola or vegetable oil

1 cup (125 g) all-purpose flour

16 ounces (480 ml) Renaissance Wit (or a similar beer)

2 tablespoons vegetable oil, divided

1 pound (454 g) fresh okra, sliced ½ inch (13 mm) thick

½ cup (50 g) chopped celery

1 cup (110 g) chopped yellow onion

½ cup (75 g) chopped green bell pepper

1 can (14.5 ounces, or 400 g) diced tomatoes, undrained

2 cups (480 ml) chicken stock

2 bay leaves

1 teaspoon salt

½ teaspoon dried thyme

½ teaspoon ground coriander

1 teaspoon black pepper

1 teaspoon Cajun seasoning

1 teaspoon hot sauce (I recommend Sylvia's Kickin' Hot, Hot Sauce)

1 pound (454 g) lump crabmeat

1. In a large skillet, heat the ½ cup (120 ml) oil over medium heat. Add the flour and cook, stirring frequently, for 30 to 40 minutes, until browned. Stir in the beer.

2. While the roux cooks, heat 1 tablespoon of the vegetable oil in a large pot over medium-high heat. Add the okra and cook and stir until golden brown, about 4 to 5 minutes. Remove the okra from the pot and transfer to a small bowl.

3. Heat the remaining 1 tablespoon oil in the same pot. Add the celery, onion, and bell pepper and cook and stir for 2 minutes.

4. Add the cooked roux, tomatoes and their juice, stock, bay leaves, salt, thyme, coriander, black pepper, Cajun seasoning, and hot sauce, along with the cooked okra, and stir to combine. Bring to a boil, then reduce the heat to low and let simmer for 45 minutes, uncovered.

5. Stir in the crabmeat and parsley and let simmer for 3 minutes. Add the shrimp and cook for 2 minutes, or until it turns mostly pink. Add the oysters and their liquor and cook until the oysters' edges start to curl, 2 to 3 minutes.

6. Remove and discard the bay leaves and serve with rice.

2 tablespoons chopped fresh parsley

1 pound (454 g) medium-size raw shrimp, peeled and deveined

1 pint (600 ml) freshly shucked oysters, with their liquor

Cooked rice, for serving

CHEESY BREWSY SOUP

As you savor each cheesy spoonful, you'll experience a perfect blend of the hearty warmth of the soup and the refreshing undertones of the wheat beer.

SERVES 4

2 tablespoons unsalted butter

1 cup (110 g) finely chopped onion

2 ribs celery, finely chopped

2 cloves garlic, minced

6 ounces (180 ml) Renaissance Wit (or a similar beer)

1 cup (240 ml) chicken broth

18 ounces (500 g) shredded Cheddar cheese

2 cups (480 ml) heavy cream

3 tablespoons all-purpose flour

Salt and black pepper (optional)

½ cup (75 g) cooked cubed ham, bacon, or turkey, for topping

1. In a large pot, melt the butter over medium heat. Add the onion, celery, and garlic and cook and stir until the vegetables are tender, 3 to 5 minutes.

2. Slowly stir in the beer and broth. Bring to the boil over medium-high heat and stir. Reduce the heat to medium-low, then add the cheese and cream, stirring to combine and cooking until the cheese is completely melted.

3. In a small bowl, whisk the flour with 3 tablespoons of water until smooth. Add this roux to the pot, stir thoroughly, and cook for an additional 5 minutes. Season with salt and pepper, if desired.

4. Ladle into bowls and serve with the ham, bacon, or turkey for topping.

WHISKEY-INFUSED SHRIMP BEERISQUE

This recipe adds a spirited twist to the classic shrimp bisque. Each spoonful offers a tantalizing blend of seafood excellence and the distinctive notes of Sugar Hill Golden Ale and whiskey. Get ready to savor a bisque that's as comforting as it is thrilling!

SERVES 6

¼ cup (60 ml) olive oil

2 medium onions, chopped

2 ribs celery, chopped

2 medium carrots, chopped

4 cloves garlic, minced

2 medium tomatoes, chopped

1 can (8 ounces, or 227 g) tomato sauce

¼ cup (10 g) finely chopped fresh cilantro

1 tablespoon brown sugar

3 pounds (1.4 kg) medium-size raw shrimp, shells on and deveined

1 tablespoon smoked paprika

1 tablespoon kosher salt

1 tablespoon black pepper

12 ounces (360 ml) Renaissance Wit (or a similar beer)

1 shot (45 ml) whiskey (I like Uncle Nearest 1856)

1 cup (240 ml) heavy cream

Cooked white rice, for serving (optional)

1. In a Dutch oven, heat the oil over medium heat. Add the onions, celery, and carrots and cook and stir until the vegetables are tender, about 5 minutes. Add the garlic, tomatoes, tomato sauce, cilantro, and brown sugar and cook for 5 to 7 minutes, stirring occasionally, until the brown sugar is dissolved and slightly thickened.

2. While the sauce is cooking, peel the shells off the shrimp and reserve them for making stock. To make the shrimp stock, bring 2 cups (480 ml) of water to a boil in a medium pot. Add the shrimp shells and let boil for 10 to 15 minutes. Strain the stock into a medium bowl and discard the shells.

3. Add the paprika, salt, and pepper to the Dutch oven, along with the beer and strained shrimp stock. Stir to combine and bring to a boil over medium-high heat. Reduce the heat to medium-low and let simmer for 30 minutes.

4. Stir in the shrimp and cook, stirring occasionally, for 5 to 7 minutes, until the shrimp are pink and no longer translucent. To flambé, pour the whiskey over the soup, then ignite the whiskey with a long match and let it cook out, about 30 seconds. This step is optional and can be accomplished without the flambé; just add the whiskey to the soup with the shrimp and allow it to cook off while the shrimp cooks. Stir in the cream and bring the soup to a simmer for 2 to 3 minutes over medium-low heat.

5. Serve as is or over rice, if you like.

BUTTERNUT SQUASH SOUP

Harlem Brewing teamed up with Whole Foods (97th and Columbus—where the famous Mikell's jazz club once stood) and the Jazz Foundation of America in 2010 to enjoy a taste of great music, local food, Harlem Brews, beer pairings, and heritage. During the cozy fall season, we worked with Whole Foods' culinary team to make our butternut squash soup infused with Lenox Lager on the evening of Patience Higgins and the Sugar Hill Quartet's performance. Best pairing ever!

SERVES 4

---

1 large butternut squash (3 to 4 pounds, or 1.4 to 1.8 kg)

3 tablespoons olive oil, divided

1 teaspoon cayenne pepper

1 teaspoon onion powder

½ teaspoon black pepper

½ cup (55 g) chopped onion

1 tablespoon minced garlic

6 ounces (180 ml) Lenox Lager (or a similar beer)

2 tablespoons honey

1 teaspoon ground cinnamon or nutmeg

1. Preheat the oven to 375°F (190°C).

2. Slice the squash in half lengthwise and scoop out and discard the seeds. Place the squash halves on a baking sheet, cut sides up, and coat the cut sides of the squash with 1 tablespoon of the oil. Evenly sprinkle the halves with the cayenne, onion powder, and black pepper.

3. Roast until fork-tender, about 45 minutes. Let cool a bit, then scoop out the squash flesh and transfer it to a blender.

4. In a small skillet, heat the remaining 2 tablespoons oil over medium heat. Add the onion and garlic and cook and stir until the onion is tender, 3 to 5 minutes.

5. Transfer the cooked onion and garlic to the blender, along with the beer, honey, and cinnamon. Process until smooth and creamy.

6. Pour the contents of the blender into a large saucepan and heat over medium heat, stirring frequently, until hot, 7 to 10 minutes.

7. Ladle into bowls and serve hot.

FISH & POULTRY

CEREMONY

Growing up, Kwanzaa was an annual community celebration and feast. We'd gather as a family with friends at the local library to honor our ancestors through African and American traditions, lighting candles for each principle, enjoying live music, sharing spoken word, and sipping on Mom's homemade ginger beer inspired by our family friends, Barbara and Musa Karmara. And we ate her peanut butter chicken, which was off-the-bone good!

My first brewing experience was helping Mom make the annual ginger beer for Kwanzaa. For days, I fell asleep with ginger beer aromas in my bedroom; ginger and cinnamon took over the house, along with the peanut butter chicken dish. Peanut butter and jelly was the sandwich in our lunch boxes, so when Mom used every spoonful of peanut butter for the chicken, I couldn't believe it. But it was so delicious, my stomach didn't fuss!

FISH FRY BEER-BATTERED CATFISH

The week before a family reunion, we would gather our fishing rods and worms for bait to catch as many fish as possible for the big fish fry. We caught catfish, carp, shad, and brim, and bought porgies and croakers from the market! Grandma Ruby would wash the carp in vinegar, season it with salt and pepper, and batter and fry it until golden brown. She would then serve it with a side of hot corn bread. This dish pays homage to our family reunions, combining the delicate taste of catfish with a crisp beer batter infused with zesty lemon pepper. Get ready to savor the crispy exterior and succulent interior of this classic Southern favorite that captures the heart and soul of down-home cooking.

SERVES 4

1 cup (125 g) all-purpose flour

1 cup (135 g) medium yellow cornmeal

1 teaspoon lemon pepper

½ teaspoon salt

½ teaspoon paprika

1 cup (240 ml) Route 64 Lager (or a similar beer, preferably a light lager)

Vegetable oil, for frying

4 catfish fillets (or bone-in if desired)

Lemon wedges, for serving

1. In a large bowl, combine the flour, cornmeal, lemon pepper, salt, and paprika and mix well.

2. Slowly pour in the beer while whisking to create a smooth batter; the consistency should be thick enough to coat the catfish but not too dense.

3. Heat about 2 inches (5 cm) of vegetable oil in a deep fryer or large deep skillet to 350°F (175°C).

4. Pat the catfish fillets dry with paper towels. Dredge each fillet in the beer batter, ensuring it is thoroughly coated.

5. Carefully place the battered catfish fillets into the hot oil, working in batches to avoid overcrowding. Fry for 4 to 6 minutes per side, until golden brown and the fish flakes easily with a fork. Transfer to a paper towel–lined plate to absorb excess oil and tent with aluminum foil to keep warm while you fry the remaining fillets.

6. Serve hot with lemon wedges for squeezing.

LOBSTER IN BEER CREAM SAUCE

This recipe combines succulent lobster meat with a sauce that's a dynamic duo of beer notes and creamy decadence.

SERVES 4

---

4 lobster tails

¼ cup (60 ml) olive oil

2 tablespoons minced garlic

1 tablespoon finely chopped fresh thyme leaves

1 tablespoon finely chopped fresh cilantro

3 ounces (90 ml) Renaissance Wit (or a similar beer)

1 cup (240 g) diced tomatoes

½ cup (120 ml) heavy cream

Salt and black pepper

Cooked rice or pasta, for serving

1. Cut the lobster tails in half, then rinse them thoroughly and pat dry with paper towels.

2. In a large skillet, heat the oil over medium heat. Add the lobster and cook for 3 to 5 minutes, flipping halfway through until the shells are red and the meat is no longer translucent.

3. Add the garlic, thyme, and cilantro and stir. Add the beer and diced tomatoes, cover the skillet with the lid, and let cook for 10 minutes. Remove the lobster from the pan and let cool.

4. Add the cream to the skillet and cook, stirring occasionally, for 3 minutes. Crack the cooled lobster tails, remove the meat, and add it to the sauce. Season with salt and pepper.

5. Serve over rice or pasta.

BUTTERMILK BEER FRIED OYSTERS

You've gotta try this irresistible creation in which briny oysters are soaked in a rich beer and buttermilk marinade and then fried until crisp and golden for unbelievable taste and texture.

SERVES 4

---

1 pound (454 g) shucked oysters

4 ounces (120 ml) Queen Stout (or a similar beer)

½ cup (120 ml) buttermilk

1 cup (240 ml) canola or vegetable oil, for frying

¼ teaspoon cayenne pepper

¼ teaspoon onion powder

1 teaspoon sea salt

½ cup (90 g) cornmeal

½ cup (65 g) all-purpose flour

Spicy Brewmoulade (page 160), for serving

1. Drain the oysters but do not rinse.

2. Add the beer and buttermilk to a medium bowl and stir to combine. Add the oysters to the bowl and let marinate in the refrigerator for 20 minutes.

3. Meanwhile, in a large skillet, preferably cast iron, heat the oil over medium-high heat.

4. In a separate medium bowl, combine the cayenne, onion powder, salt, cornmeal, and flour and stir well.

5. Dip each oyster in the flour mixture, then, working in batches so as not to overcrowd the oil, cook in the hot skillet for 3 minutes, or until browned and crispy. Transfer to a paper towel–lined plate to absorb any excess oil.

6. Serve with the spicy brewmoulade for dipping.

MUSSELS IN STOUT CREAM SAUCE

This dish by Chef Malik combines the delicate allure of fresh mussels with the robust sophistication of a velvety stout-infused cream sauce, creating layers of flavors.

SERVES 1

---

16 mussels

¼ cup (60 ml) vegetable or avocado oil

1 tablespoon salt

½ tablespoon black pepper

2 tablespoons fresh lemon juice

½ cup (120 ml) Queen Stout Brewduction (page 160)

1 cup (240 ml) heavy cream

1 tablespoon finely chopped fresh parsley

¼ cup (15 g) chopped scallion, for garnishing

1. Clean the mussels by removing their beards under cold water.

2. In a large skillet, heat the oil over medium-high heat, about 45 seconds. Add the mussels to the skillet and cook and stir until they begin to open, about 2 minutes.

3. Add the salt, pepper, and lemon juice to the pan. Stir in the brewduction and cream and cook for 3 minutes, or until the cream reduces and thickens.

4. Transfer the mussels to a serving platter, leaving the sauce in the skillet. Discard any mussels whose shells have not opened. Taste the sauce and make sure it is thick and creamy and can coat the back of a spoon.

5. Turn off the heat, then stir in the parsley.

6. Pour the sauce over the mussels and garnish with the chopped scallion.

SAVOY BAKED SALMON

This marvelous dish swings with the richness of fresh salmon fillets and a marinade made with Renaissance Wit, producing a delicious fusion of tastes and textures.

SERVES 4

---

8 ounces (240 ml) Renaissance Wit (or a similar beer)

2 teaspoons olive oil, plus more for greasing

3 cloves garlic, minced

1 teaspoon dried thyme

1 teaspoon paprika

1 teaspoon onion powder

Salt and black pepper

4 salmon fillets

Chopped fresh parsley, for garnishing

Lemon wedges, for serving

1. In a large bowl, combine the beer, oil, garlic, thyme, paprika, and onion powder. Season with salt and pepper and blend well.

2. Add the salmon fillets to the bowl and coat them with the beerinade. Cover and let marinate in the refrigerator for at least 30 minutes and up to 2 hours.

3. Preheat the oven to 375°F (190°C). Grease a 9 x 13-inch (23 x 33 cm) baking dish with olive oil.

4. Transfer the marinated fillets to the prepared baking dish.

5. Bake for 18 to 20 minutes, until the salmon flakes effortlessly with a fork. If desired, for the final 2 to 3 minutes of baking, turn the oven to broil if you want a crispy top.

6. Garnish with the chopped parsley and serve with the lemon wedges for squeezing.

CRABBIE CAKES

The family reunion at Baltimore Harbor was one of our all-time favorites. We ate crabs until sundown with bottoms up. These tantalizing, spicy, beer-infused crab cakes, a fusion of succulent crabmeat, bold spices, and the rich flavors of lager, pay homage to that memorable experience.

SERVES 4

1 pound (454 g) lump crabmeat, picked over for pieces of shell

4 ounces (120 ml) Lenox Lager (or a similar beer)

½ cup (120 ml) mayonnaise

1 tablespoon Dijon mustard

1 tablespoon Worcestershire sauce

2 teaspoons Old Bay seasoning

1 teaspoon hot sauce, or to taste

1 cup (100 g) bread crumbs

¼ cup (15 g) finely chopped scallion

¼ cup (13 g) finely chopped fresh parsley

Salt and black pepper

2 eggs, beaten

Vegetable oil, for frying

Favorite dipping sauce, for serving

1. In a large bowl, combine the crabmeat, beer, mayonnaise, Dijon mustard, Worcestershire sauce, Old Bay seasoning, hot sauce, bread crumbs, scallion, and parsley. Mix gently to preserve the crabmeat's texture.

2. Season the mixture with salt and pepper, then add the beaten eggs and mix until well combined.

3. Form crab cakes into ⅓-cup portions, shaping them into even patties.

4. In a large skillet, heat the oil over medium-high heat. Once hot, working in batches, fry the crab cakes until golden brown on both sides, 3 to 4 minutes per side. Transfer to a paper towel–lined plate to absorb excess oil.

5. Serve hot with your favorite dipping sauce.

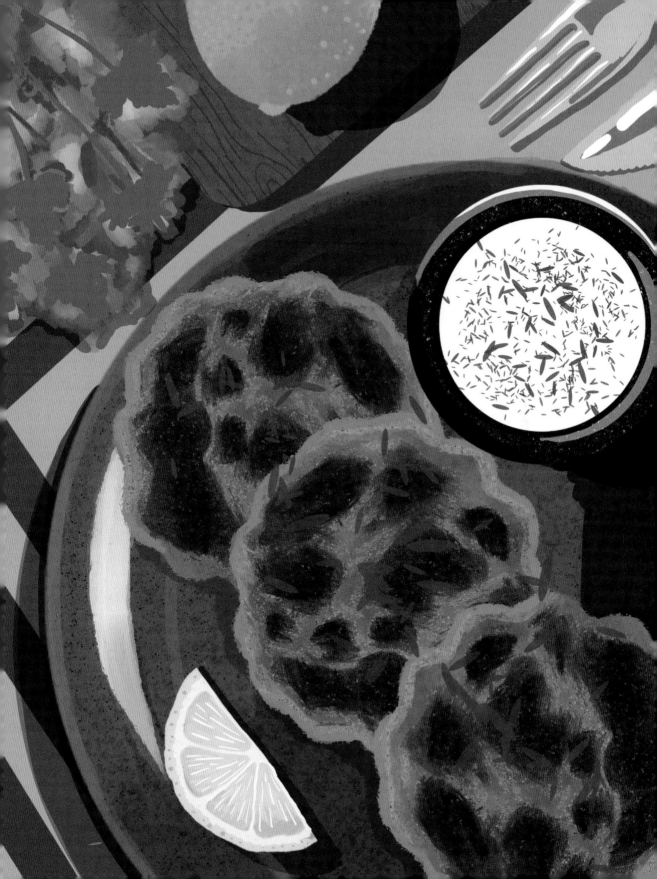

NOT MY MOMMA'S PEANUT BUTTER CHICKEN

This culinary masterpiece is a homegrown Kwanzaa favorite, combining succulent chicken thighs with a luscious peanut butter sauce, elevated by Sugar Hill Golden Ale, which imparts a subtle depth of flavor. Each tender piece of chicken marinates in a medley of soy sauce, garlic, ginger, and aromatic spices, laying the groundwork for a culinary ride on the A Train!

SERVES 4 TO 6

¼ cup (60 ml) soy sauce

3 tablespoons olive oil, divided

4 cloves garlic, minced

1 tablespoon finely chopped fresh ginger

1 teaspoon red pepper flakes, or to taste

1 teaspoon ground coriander

Salt and black pepper

1½ pounds (680 g) boneless, skinless chicken thighs, cut into bite-size pieces

1 cup (240 ml) creamy peanut butter

8 ounces (240 ml) Sugar Hill Golden Ale (or a similar beer)

1 tablespoon honey

Chopped peanuts, for garnishing

Sliced scallion, for garnishing

Cooked noodles or rice, for serving

1. In a large bowl, combine the soy sauce, 1 tablespoon of the olive oil, the garlic, ginger, red pepper flakes, and coriander. Season with salt and pepper and mix well. Add the chicken pieces, coat thoroughly with the marinade, cover the bowl, and refrigerate for at least 15 minutes and up to 6 hours.

2. In a large skillet, heat the remaining 2 tablespoons oil over medium-high heat. Add the chicken to the skillet and cook until browned, 5 to 7 minutes per side.

3. While the chicken is cooking, combine the peanut butter, beer, and honey in a medium bowl and whisk until smooth.

4. Pour the peanut butter mixture over the cooked chicken in the skillet. Reduce the heat to medium-low and let simmer for 15 to 20 minutes, until the chicken is thoroughly cooked and the sauce is thickened.

5. Garnish with the chopped peanuts and scallion and serve with noodles or cooked rice.

DOWN-HOME BEER-SMOTHERED CHICKEN

This recipe, one of my family's favorites, is an homage to Southern comfort. Tender chicken bathed in a beer-infused gravy will transport you to the welcoming kitchens of Eastern Carolina, where each bite tells a story steeped in culinary heritage. Gravy rules!

SERVES 4 TO 6

6 bone-in, skin-on chicken thighs, fat trimmed

6 ounces (180 ml) Renaissance Wit or beer of choice

1 teaspoon black pepper

1 teaspoon smoked paprika

1 teaspoon garlic powder

1 teaspoon dried cilantro

1 teaspoon dried rosemary

1 teaspoon salt

1 cup (125 g) all-purpose flour

2 tablespoons neutral oil, for frying

½ cup (55 g) chopped onion

½ cup (75 g) chopped green bell pepper

2 cups (480 ml) chicken broth

Rice, for serving

1. In a medium bowl, marinate the chicken in the beer, covered, in the refrigerator for 2 hours.

2. Remove the chicken from the beer and pat dry with paper towels, reserving the beerinade.

3. In a shallow dish, combine the black pepper, paprika, garlic powder, cilantro, rosemary, and salt and mix well. Place the flour in a separate shallow dish.

4. First, coat the chicken thighs on both sides with the spice blend, then do the same in the flour. Reserve 2 tablespoons of the flour and mix with the remaining spice mixture.

5. In a large skillet, heat the oil over medium heat. Once the oil is hot, add the chicken, skin sides down, and cook for 4 minutes, then flip over and cook for another 4 minutes, until golden and crispy. Transfer to a plate.

6. To the same skillet, add the onion and bell pepper. Reduce the heat to medium and cook and stir for 3 to 5 minutes, until the vegetables begin to become tender and lightly browned.

7. Add the reserved seasoned flour and stir to coat the vegetables. Add the reserved beerinade and stir until thickened and creamy, about 2 minutes. Add the broth, bring the mixture to a boil, and then add back the chicken thighs, skin sides up. Reduce the heat to medium-low and let simmer for 7 minutes.

8. Spoon some gravy over the chicken and serve over rice.

BRILLED BEER CAN CHICKEN

This is hands down one of our favorite chicken dishes! The Cajun-spiced, tender brewsy juiciness of the chicken does not disappoint.

SERVES 4 TO 6

1 roasting chicken (about 4 pounds, or 1.8 kg)

1 tablespoon olive oil

3 tablespoons Cajun seasoning, divided

1 can (12 ounces, or 360 ml) Lenox Lager (or a similar beer)

1. Set up a grill, whether charcoal or gas, with heat on one side, so the chicken will not be over direct heat. Preheat to medium.

2. Rub the chicken on all sides with the oil, then sprinkle the skin evenly with 2 tablespoons of the Cajun seasoning.

3. Pour about half of the beer into a glass and enjoy it while you cook chicken. Remove any labels from the beer can, if possible, then make two or three additional holes in the top of the beer can with a church-key can opener. Add the remaining 1 tablespoon Cajun seasoning to the can (the beer may foam when you add the seasoning).

4. On a flat work surface, gently place the chicken cavity onto the beer can and spread out the legs, adjusting them until two are in the front of the can and the other two are in the back, to form a stable balance. Tuck the wing tips behind the chicken's back.

5. Place the chicken along with the beer can on the grill, but not over direct heat. Bring the cover down on the grill and allow to cook for 1 to 1½ hours, until the chicken reaches an internal temperature of 165°F (74°C). Remove the chicken, with the can still in place, from the grill, tent with aluminum foil, and allow to rest for 15 minutes.

6. Carefully remove the beer can from the cavity and carve the chicken. Serve hot.

BEER FRIED CHICKEN AND WAFFLES

According to historical research, the modern version of chicken and waffles was first served in Harlem at Well's Supper Club as early as the 1930s. So, of course, we had to give this iconic culinary marriage a brewlicious twist!

SERVES 4

BEER FRIED CHICKEN

1½ cups (190 g) all-purpose flour

1 tablespoon paprika

1 tablespoon black pepper

1 tablespoon onion powder

1 tablespoon garlic powder

1 tablespoon dried cilantro

½ tablespoon salt

2 large eggs

6 ounces (180 ml) Grapricot Hefeweizen (or a similar beer)

1 cup (240 ml) neutral oil, for frying

1½ pounds (680 g) chicken wings

WAFFLES

2 cups (250 g) all-purpose flour

2 tablespoons sugar

2 teaspoons baking powder

1 teaspoon baking soda

½ teaspoon salt

2 large eggs, separated

1¾ cups (420 ml) buttermilk

1. **To make the beer fried chicken:** In a medium bowl, combine the 1½ cups (190 g) flour, paprika, pepper, onion powder, garlic powder, cilantro, and salt and blend well.

2. In a separate medium bowl, whisk together the eggs and beer.

3. In a large skillet, heat the 1 cup (240 ml) neutral oil over medium heat until it reaches about 375°F (190°C). Dip each chicken wing in the egg-beer batter, then coat it in the seasoned flour. Working in batches, fry the wings, while not overcrowding the pan, until golden brown and crispy, 8 to 10 minutes. Transfer to a paper towel–lined plate to absorb excess oil.

4. **To make the waffles:** Preheat a waffle iron according to the manufacturer's instructions.

5. In a large bowl, whisk together the flour, sugar, baking powder, baking soda, and salt until well blended. In a medium bowl, lightly beat the egg yolks. Stir in the buttermilk, beer, and melted butter until smooth. Gradually pour the wet ingredients into the dry ingredients, stirring until just combined. Be careful not to overmix; a few lumps are fine.

6. In a separate large bowl, beat the egg whites until stiff peaks form. Gently fold the beaten egg whites into the batter; this will help make the waffles airy and light.

7. Lightly grease the preheated waffle iron with butter. Pour some batter onto the center of the waffle iron, spreading it evenly to the edges. Close the lid and cook

6 ounces (180 ml) Sugar Hill Golden Ale (or a similar beer)

¼ cup (60 g) unsalted butter, melted, plus more for greasing

Maple syrup, for serving (optional)

the waffles according to the manufacturer's instructions, or until golden brown and crispy. Carefully remove the cooked waffle from the iron and place it on a wire rack to cool slightly or serve immediately. Repeat with the remaining batter, greasing the iron as needed.

8. Serve the waffles topped with the beer fried chicken wings and maple syrup (if using).

BEEF, PORK & LAMB

UNCLE PRODIGAL'S SUN

Uncle Prodigal and his beloved Sweetie reigned as culinary maestros in the quaint town of Cope, South Carolina. As the brother of the indomitable Grandma Ruby, Uncle Prodigal's farm teemed with life, from the playful antics of pigs and chickens to the bustling trade of freshly laid eggs.

But it wasn't just the farm that brimmed with activity; it was the kitchen, where Sweetie's cast-iron skillet danced over the stove. With a flair for gaming, the couple elevated their breakfasts and dinners to epic proportions, transforming humble ingredients into culinary masterpieces.

As the summer sun painted the landscape in hues of gold, my mother, a mere eight years old, took an annual pilgrimage with her kin to Spartanburg, South Carolina, with their destination being the cotton fields, where each pluck of the fluffy, white bolls promised a few hard-earned dollars. Yet, despite the toil, there was a sense of camaraderie as the family worked all day under the Southern sky, their laughter mingling with the rustle of leaves.

But it wasn't just cotton that filled their days; it was the thrill of the hunt. Through the dense woods, they ventured, chasing rabbits, squirrels, and mischievous raccoons, their bounty a testament to the land's generosity. And when game proved elusive, Uncle Prodigal's ingenuity knew no bounds as he cast bread crumbs into the edgewater, coaxing forth fish to grace the dinner table.

Amid the hustle and bustle of farm life, Aunt Sweetie made magic with her cast-iron skillet, seasoned to perfection with generations of love. The aroma of freshly baked corn bread mingled with the sizzle of streaks of lean pork bacon, the flavors dancing upon the palate. And as the sun reached its zenith, homemade lemonade was kept cool in a galvanized tub, a refreshing respite from the heat of the day.

HAMBREWGER CASSEROLE

This filling, simple-to-make casserole combines a hearty lager with the rich flavors of ground beef, diced tomatoes, and tomato sauce. Seasoned with oregano and basil and topped with a thick layer of melted Cheddar, this tasty dish is guaranteed to become a weekly favorite.

SERVES 6 TO 8

---

2 pounds (907 g) ground beef

1 medium onion, finely chopped

2 cloves garlic, minced

1 can (14.5 ounces, or 411 g) diced tomatoes

1 can (8 ounces, or 227 g) tomato sauce

1 can (6 ounces, or 170 g) tomato paste

8 ounces (240 ml) Lenox Lager (or a similar beer)

1 teaspoon dried oregano

1 teaspoon dried basil

Salt and black pepper

2 cups (225 g) elbow macaroni

Nonstick cooking spray

2 cups (230 g) finely shredded Cheddar cheese

1. Preheat the oven to 375°F (190°C).

2. In a large skillet over medium heat, add the ground beef and cook, stirring, until browned, 5 to 7 minutes. Pour the meat into a colander, draining off all the fat. Do not wipe the skillet clean.

3. Place the skillet back on the stove over medium heat. Add the onion and garlic and cook and stir until the onions have softened and are translucent, about 5 minutes.

4. Add the diced tomatoes, tomato sauce, tomato paste, beer, oregano, and basil to the pan and season with salt and pepper. Stir everything together and let simmer for 10 minutes.

5. Meanwhile, cook the macaroni to al dente following the directions on the package. Drain.

6. Grease a 9 x 13-inch (23 x 33 cm) baking dish with cooking spray.

7. Add the cooked macaroni and beef-tomato mixture to a large bowl and mix to coat the pasta. Pour the mixture into the prepared baking dish and sprinkle the Cheddar cheese evenly over the top.

8. Bake for 20 minutes, or until the cheese is bubbling and melted. Remove from the oven and give it a few minutes to cool before serving.

SMASH BREWGERS

Chef Malik's juicy, flavorful smash burgers are a celebration of simplicity and indulgence, with each bite promising unapologetic savory goodness and a hint of hops. Get ready to experience the ultimate burger sensation with a delightful beer-infused twist!

MAKES 10 BURGERS

---

8 ounces (240 ml) Renaissance Wit (or a similar beer)

3 pounds (1.4 kg) ground beef (80% lean/20% fat)

1 tablespoon salt, plus more for seasoning

1½ tablespoons coarse-ground black pepper, plus more for seasoning

2 tablespoons garlic powder

10 hamburger buns

Toppings of choice, for serving

1. In a medium pot, cook the beer over medium-high heat until it reduces by one-third. Let cool.

2. In a medium bowl, combine the beef, salt, pepper, garlic powder, and beer reduction and mix well.

3. Form the burgers into 5-ounce (142 g) patties to make about 10 patties. Press each patty as flat as possible to make a true smash burger.

4. Heat a large skillet over medium-high heat. Season each patty with a pinch of salt and pepper on both sides.

5. Working in batches, add the patties to the hot pan and cook for 2 minutes on each side, or until cooked to the desired doneness. (If you want to make a cheeseburger, add the cheese after you flip them.)

6. Serve on buns with all your favorite burger toppings.

MARVTASTIC BRISKET

This recipe is dedicated to Larry Leon Hamlin, "Mr. Marvtastic," a family friend and master of theater. When there's no word to describe how great something is, it's "marvtastic," a word created and popularized by Mr. Hamlin himself. Immerse yourself in the richness of this brisket, with its layers of flavors from the beer, brown sugar, garlic, and onion, which will resonate deep within your soul.

SERVES 8

---

1 beef brisket (about 6 pounds, or 2.7 kg), with ¼ inch (6 mm) of fat left on

2 tablespoons black pepper

¼ cup garlic powder

2 tablespoons onion powder

2 tablespoons paprika

1 tablespoon seasoned salt (I recommend Sylvia's Soulful Seasoned Salt)

1 large onion, chopped

12 ounces (360 ml) Sugar Hill Golden Ale (or a similar beer)

1 tablespoon dark brown sugar

2 tablespoons soy or Worcestershire sauce

1. Preheat the oven to 375°F (190°C). Place the brisket in a roasting pan.

2. In a medium bowl, combine the pepper, garlic powder, onion powder, paprika, and seasoned salt and stir well. Sprinkle the seasoning all over the brisket and rub it in. Spread the chopped onions all over the brisket.

3. Place the brisket, fat side up, in the roasting pan.

4. In a small bowl, combine the beer, brown sugar, and soy or Worcestershire sauce and mix well. Pour the mixture around the brisket and cover the pan with the lid.

5. Roast for 1½ hours. Remove the brisket from the oven and baste with the juices. Cover again and return it to the oven. Roast for another 1½ hours, or until a knife inserted in the center comes out easily. Let cool for 10 to 15 minutes, then carve into thin slices.

6. To serve, place the sliced brisket on a platter and serve with the pan juices.

BEEF CURRY

This is hands down one of my favorite recipes. It combines tender chunks of beef, vibrant spices, and the distinctive hoppy notes of our Rocky Mount Hazy IPA, creating a curry experience like no other. Whether you're a curry enthusiast or a newcomer to the world of spice, this dish promises to delight your taste buds.

SERVES 4

---

2 pounds (907 g) stewing beef, cut into 2-inch (5 cm) cubes

¼ cup (60 ml) Curry Sauce (page 163)

1 crushed red chili pepper

5 tablespoons neutral oil

2 onions, sliced

2 tomatoes, chopped

1 pint (600 ml) coconut milk, plus more if needed

6 ounces (180 ml) Common Threads Pineapple & Hibiscus Pale Ale (or a similar beer)

4 teaspoons sugar

2 chives

½ teaspoon salt

¼ cup (35 g) raisins

Cooked basmati or another long-grain rice, for serving

1. In a large bowl, mix the beef with the curry sauce and chili pepper.

2. In a large skillet, heat the oil over medium heat. Add the meat and onions and cook for 4 minutes, or until the meat is browned on all sides. Stir in the tomatoes, cover the pan with the lid, and let cook for 20 minutes, or until the liquid is almost all absorbed.

3. Remove the lid from the pan. Add the coconut milk, beer, sugar, chives, and salt, reduce the heat to medium-low and let cook for 1 hour. At this point, check to make sure there is enough liquid. If there is not enough liquid, add 1 cup (240 ml) of water to the pan along with the raisins, cover again, and cook for an additional 30 minutes, or until the beef is tender.

4. Serve hot over rice.

SWEET HOME MEAT LOAF

This twist on a family favorite layers the sweet malt flavors of 125th Street IPA with a medley of spices, evoking nostalgia and culinary delight with every bite.

SERVES 6 TO 8

MEAT LOAF

½ cup (120 ml) whole milk

4 ounces (120 ml) 125th Street IPA (or a similar beer)

1½ cups (135 g) crushed soda crackers

½ cup (65 g) finely chopped sweet onion

⅓ cup (50 g) finely chopped green bell pepper

1 teaspoon salt

½ teaspoon celery salt

½ teaspoon paprika

½ teaspoon black pepper

1½ cups (170 g) shredded Cheddar cheese

2 large eggs

1 pound (454 g) ground beef (85% lean/15% fat)

1 pound (454 g) ground pork

GLAZE

2 tablespoons Queen Stout (or a similar beer)

½ cup (120 ml) molasses

½ cup (120 ml) ketchup

1. Preheat the oven to 375°F (190°C). Line a baking sheet with parchment.

2. **To make the meat loaf:** In a large bowl, combine the milk, IPA beer, and soda crackers and stir to incorporate. Let soak for 10 minutes.

3. Add the onion, bell pepper, salt, celery salt, paprika, pepper, Cheddar, eggs, beef, and pork to the bowl with the soaked crackers. Mix until thoroughly combined, but do not overmix; this will result in a tough meat loaf.

4. **To make the glaze:** In a small bowl, whisk together the stout beer, molasses, and ketchup.

5. Transfer the meat mixture to the prepared baking sheet and form into a loaf, approximately 10 x 4 inches (25 x 10 cm).

6. Drizzle half the glaze on top of the meat loaf and spread to coat.

7. Bake for 45 minutes, or until a meat thermometer inserted into the center registers 160°F (71°C).

8. Remove from the oven and baste the hot meat loaf with the remaining glaze. Let sit for 10 minutes before slicing.

9. Slice and serve.

BEERINATED LAMB CHOPS

Any time a lamb dish was served for dinner, it most often was for a special occasion. These lamb chops are divine when marinated in the deep, malty notes of Queen Stout and accompanied by the aromatic embrace of rosemary, the warmth of cumin, and the tanginess of minced garlic.

SERVES 4

2 tablespoons soy sauce

4 ounces (120 ml) Queen Stout (or a similar beer)

8 lamb loin chops

½ teaspoon dried rosemary or finely chopped fresh rosemary

½ teaspoon black pepper

¼ teaspoon ground cumin

½ teaspoon garlic powder

½ teaspoon salt

3 tablespoons neutral oil

1 tablespoon unsalted butter

2 cloves garlic, minced

¼ cup (35 g) finely chopped onion

2 tablespoons mint jelly, for serving

1. In a large bowl, combine the soy sauce and beer and stir well. Add the lamb chops to the bowl, making sure they are completely covered with the beerinade. Let marinate in the refrigerator, covered, for 6 to 24 hours. Remove the chops from the beerinade, reserving the beerinade, and pat them dry.

2. In a small bowl, combine the rosemary, black pepper, cumin, garlic powder, and salt and mix well. Season the lamb chops with the spice mixture.

3. In a large skillet, heat the oil over medium-high heat. Add the chops to the pan and sear on both sides until browned and cooked to desired doneness, 3 to 5 minutes on each side. Remove the chops from the pan.

4. Reduce the heat to medium and add the butter to the skillet. Once melted, add the garlic and onion and cook and stir for 2 minutes. Add the reserved beerinade and allow to boil for 2 minutes, stirring frequently.

5. Add the lamb chops back to the pan and thoroughly coat them with the sauce. Serve hot with the mint jelly.

BREWSY PULLED PORK

This mouthwatering dish has a tender pork shoulder or butt that is marinated in a flavorful mixture of spices, slow-cooked to tenderness, and enhanced with the strong flavor of an IPA. The outcome is a delicious combination of melt-in-your-mouth meat and malty, citrusy beer flavors, making for a very fulfilling eating experience.

SERVES 12

1 teaspoon smoked paprika

1 teaspoon ground cumin

1 teaspoon onion powder

1 teaspoon garlic powder

1 teaspoon chili powder

Salt and black pepper

3 to 4 pounds (1.4 to 1.8 kg) boneless pork butt or shoulder, extra fat removed

2 teaspoons vegetable oil

1 large onion, finely chopped

3 cloves garlic, minced

12 ounces (360 ml) 125th Street IPA (or a similar beer)

1 cup (240 ml) barbecue sauce, plus more for serving

¼ cup (60 ml) apple cider vinegar

2 tablespoons brown sugar

Hamburger buns, for serving

1. In a small bowl, combine the paprika, cumin, onion powder, garlic powder, and chili powder. Season with salt and pepper and blend well.

2. Rub the pork all over with the spice mixture, making sure it is evenly coated.

3. In a large skillet, heat the oil over medium-high heat. Add the pork and sear until browned on all sides, about 5 minutes per side. Remove the pork and set on a plate to catch all the juices.

4. To the same skillet, add the onion and garlic and cook and stir until the onion has softened and is translucent, about 5 minutes. (You can scrape up all the browned bits from searing the meat, adding to the sautéed onions and garlic.)

5. Transfer the pork, onion, and garlic to a 5½- or 7-quart (5 or 6.5 L) Dutch oven or slow cooker. Add the beer, barbecue sauce, apple cider vinegar, and brown sugar.

6. If using the stovetop or a slow cooker, cover, cook over low heat or on the low setting for 4 to 6 hours, until the pork is fork-tender. If using the oven, preheat it to 325°F (165°C), then cook, covered, for 4 to 6 hours, until fork-tender.

7. Shred the pork with two forks and make sandwiches with the hamburger buns. Serve with more barbecue sauce for topping.

BEERAISED SHORT RIBS

These fall-off-the-bone short ribs are infused with the rich, sweet, malty notes of 125th Street IPA, promising an unforgettable home-cooked dining experience.

SERVES 4

---

2 tablespoons unsalted butter

2 tablespoons olive oil

¼ cup (30 g) all-purpose flour

¾ teaspoon salt

½ teaspoon black pepper

6 pounds (2.7 kg) lean, meaty short ribs

1 onion, peeled and left whole

8 whole cloves

2 bay leaves

2 cloves garlic, smashed

1 teaspoon dried rosemary

3 medium carrots, peeled and roughly chopped

1 medium turnip, quartered

4 ounces (120 ml) Queen Stout (or a similar beer)

1. In a large Dutch oven, heat the butter and oil over medium-high heat.

2. On a plate, combine the flour, salt, and pepper. Dredge the ribs in the seasoned flour, then add them to the hot oil and brown them for 3 to 5 minutes on each side.

3. To stud the onion, pierce it with the cloves and add it to the Dutch oven. Add the bay leaves, garlic, rosemary, carrots, turnip, and enough water to cover everything. Bring to a boil over medium-high heat, then reduce the heat to medium-low. Cover the pan and let gently simmer for 1 hour.

4. Add the beer and continue cooking for another hour, or until the ribs are thoroughly tender and permeated with the various flavors.

NOTE: *You can add potatoes to the pot during the last hour of cooking, if you like, or serve the braised ribs with buttered noodles.*

NOT MY DAD'S SALISBEERY STEAK

My dad enjoyed a good lager, especially with his buddies while serving as a cook in the army in Germany, and he loved cooking his signature, delectable, tender Salisbury steak recipe for our family. But this is not our dad's Salisbury steak, with the unexpected twist of lager.

SERVES 4

½ cup (50 g) bread crumbs

½ onion, peeled

1 pound (454 g) ground beef

2 cloves garlic, minced, divided

1 egg

2 ounces (60 ml) Lenox Lager (or a similar beer)

2 tablespoons ketchup

2 tablespoons neutral oil

½ cup (65 g) finely chopped onion

½ cup (35 g) thinly sliced white button mushrooms

2 tablespoons butter

2 tablespoons all-purpose flour

2 cups (480 ml) beef broth

½ teaspoon salt, plus more if needed

½ teaspoon black pepper, plus more if needed

1. Place the bread crumbs in a large bowl. Using a box grater, grate the onion half over the bread crumbs. Mix together, then let soak for a few minutes. Add the beef, 1 clove of the minced garlic, the egg, beer, and ketchup to the bowl and, using your hands, mix for a couple of minutes until the mixture is well combined. Divide the mixture into 4 equal pieces and pat firmly into oval steaks, around ¼ inch (6 mm) thick.

2. In a large skillet, heat the oil over medium-high heat. Add the steaks, working in batches if necessary, and cook for 1 minute, or until browned, then flip and brown the other side (they will still be raw inside) and cook for an additional minute. Transfer to a plate.

3. If the skillet looks dry, add a touch more oil. Add the chopped onion and remaining garlic and cook and stir over medium heat for 2 minutes, or until the onion is a bit translucent. Add the mushrooms and cook and stir for 2 to 3 minutes, until golden. Reduce the heat to medium, then melt the butter. Add the flour and cook for 30 seconds, stirring constantly. Gradually stir in the broth until mostly lump-free. Season with the salt and pepper.

4. Add the steaks back into the skillet along with their juices. Cook for 5 to 7 minutes, until the gravy thickens, stirring occasionally around the steaks. If the gravy thickens too quickly, add water. Transfer the steaks to a clean plate. Taste the gravy and adjust the salt and pepper if needed.

5. Serve the Salisbury steaks topped with the gravy.

BRILLED BADASS BBQ RIBS

I can't remember how my grandson Shaun and I ended up being invited to lunch with Melvin Van Peebles, but it was a very special moment. We talked about his films, and I asked him what inspired his film *Sweet Sweetback's Baadasssss Song*. The conversation was colorful, and the BBQ ribs were a hit! Here's the recipe that was inspired by the "godfather of modern Black cinema."

SERVES 6

BABY BACK RIBS

4 pounds (1.8 kg) pork loin ribs

1 tablespoon garlic salt

1 tablespoon onion salt

1 tablespoon paprika

1 teaspoon dried sage or finely chopped fresh sage

¼ teaspoon cayenne pepper

1 cup (240 ml) apple juice

½ cup (120 g) apple butter

¼ cup (60 ml) dark molasses

8 ounces (240 ml) Sugar Hill Golden Ale (or a similar beer)

½ cup (120 ml) bourbon

BBQ SAUCE

2 tablespoons molasses

1 teaspoon Tabasco sauce

2 teaspoons vinegar or fresh lemon juice

2 tablespoons prepared mustard

1 tablespoon soy sauce

1. **To make the baby back ribs:** Trim all the fat from the ribs. Sprinkle both sides of the ribs with the garlic salt, onion salt, paprika, sage, and cayenne and rub in the seasonings. Place the ribs in a pan that is large enough to accommodate the beerinade.

2. In a medium bowl, combine the apple juice, apple butter, molasses, beer, and bourbon for the beerinade. Mix well, then pour the beerinade over the ribs, cover the pan with plastic wrap, and let marinate in the refrigerator for 4 hours, turning two or three times.

3. Preheat a grill to medium-high. Remove the ribs from the pan, reserving the beerinade for basting. Place the ribs on the hot grill and cook until the meat starts to pull away from the bone, 30 to 35 minutes, brushing them with the beerinade every 10 minutes and flipping them halfway through cooking time.

4. **Meanwhile, make the BBQ sauce:** In a small bowl, combine all the sauce ingredients and mix well.

5. Serve the ribs with the BBQ sauce.

PORK MEATBALLS IN STOUT BBQ SAUCE

What truly sets these meatballs by Chef Malik apart is the rich and indulgent stout BBQ sauce. Enjoy as an appetizer, an entrée on a bed of creamy mashed potatoes, or as a sandwich on a fluffy bun.

MAKES 24 MEATBALLS

MEATBALLS

32 ounces (1 quart, or 1 L) Queen Stout (or a similar beer)

1 bay leaf

1 piece (1 inch, or 2.5 cm) cinnamon stick

1 tablespoon black peppercorns

1¾ pounds (794 g) ground pork

2 tablespoons salt

1 tablespoon finely chopped fresh thyme leaves

½ teaspoon ground cumin

1½ teaspoons garlic powder

1½ teaspoons onion powder

1 tablespoon browning and seasoning sauce

2 large eggs

2 cups (200 g) bread crumbs

STOUT BBQ SAUCE

2 cups (520 g) crushed tomatoes

1 tablespoon molasses

2 tablespoons browning and seasoning sauce

¼ cup (60 ml) apple cider vinegar

1. **To make the meatballs:** Preheat the oven to 300°F (150°C).

2. In a medium bowl, combine the beer, bay leaf, cinnamon stick, and peppercorns with 2 cups (480 ml) of water and mix well. This is the poaching liquid.

3. In a large bowl, combine the pork, salt, thyme, cumin, garlic powder, and onion powder and mix well. Add the browning sauce, followed by one egg at a time. Add the bread crumbs and mix until thoroughly incorporated. (Do not overmix or the mixture will become dense.) Form twenty-four 2-ounce (60 g) meatballs.

4. Transfer the meatballs to a 9 x 13-inch (23 x 33 cm) baking dish and pour the poaching liquid over them. Cover the pan with aluminum foil and bake for 30 minutes, or until firm and cooked through. Remove the foil and let sit for 30 minutes before removing the meatballs from the pan, but retaining the poaching liquid.

5. **To Make the stout BBQ sauce:** Add 2 cups (480 ml) of the poaching liquid from the cooked meatballs to a large skillet and cook over medium-high heat until the liquid reduces by one-third. Add the tomatoes, molasses, 2 tablespoons browning sauce, vinegar, and ¼ cup (60 ml) of water. Whisk together and let simmer over medium-low heat for 15 minutes. Remove from the heat.

6. To serve, add the poached meatballs to a large bowl and cover with the hot BBQ sauce.

SWEET THYME BEERINATED PORK CHOPS

These pork chops are marinated to perfection in beer and spices and then grilled to mouthwatering perfection. Whether you're hosting a summer barbecue or simply craving a hearty meal, these pork chops are sure to satiate.

SERVES 4

4 lean boneless pork chops, fat trimmed

2 tablespoons adobo seasoning

1 tablespoons sea salt

⅓ cup (15 g) finely chopped fresh cilantro

⅓ cup (15 g) finely chopped fresh thyme leaves

8 ounces (240 ml) Sugar Hill Golden Ale (or a similar beer)

3 tablespoons olive oil

1 teaspoon cane sugar

1. Rub the pork chops with the adobo and salt, then place in a medium bowl. Add the cilantro and thyme and pour in the beer. Refrigerate, covered, for 30 minutes to 2 hours. Remove the pork chops, reserving the beerinade.

2. Grease a nonstick stovetop grill pan with the olive oil and heat over medium heat. Add the pork chops and cook for 15 to 20 minutes, in 5-minute intervals per side, or until cooked to your liking. Remove the pork chops and place on a plate tented with foil to keep warm.

3. In a medium saucepan, add the reserved beerinade and sugar and cook over medium heat until it is reduced by half, about 5 minutes.

4. Place the pork chops on serving plates and spoon over the sauce.

BEERAISED SPARERIBS WITH BOURBON BBQ SAUCE

In Ed Wiley's words: Let's just say it's in my roots. As the son of a bona-fide BBQ master, there's nothing I love to prepare more than variations of Texas-style, slow-smoked brisket, ribs, chicken, and pork. My Houston-born daddy, legendary saxophonist Ed Wiley Jr., honed his craft during his early years as a bandleader on the Chitlin' Circuit in the 1940s through the '60s. He refused to patronize any restaurant that demanded Blacks enter through the back door, so he regularly put the pots on for his bandmates. Over time, he became just as revered for his food as he was for his soulful tenor solos. I spent many years shadowing him as he dug his pits, prepared his special blends of spices, created luscious sauces, and presented his masterpieces of succulent meats. One beautiful lesson he taught when it comes to smoking meat is just how wonderful the marriage is between barbecue and beer. And when you top it all off with a few shots of bourbon, you're in BBQ heaven!

SERVES 4

SPARERIBS

4 to 5 tablespoons kosher salt

2 tablespoons smoked paprika

2 tablespoons coarse black pepper

1 tablespoon onion powder

2 tablespoons garlic powder

1 tablespoon cayenne pepper

1 teaspoon ground cumin

2 slabs spareribs (remove the membrane on the bone side of the ribs)

48 ounces (1.4 L) Queen Stout (or a similar beer)

1. **To make the spareribs:** In a medium bowl, combine the kosher salt, paprika, black pepper, onion powder, garlic powder, cayenne, and cumin and whisk together to blend.

2. Rub the spice mixture all over both sides of the slabs of ribs. Place the spice-rubbed ribs in an oven-safe baking dish and cover them with the beer, making sure the ribs are fully submerged. Cover and refrigerate for at least 8 hours, or overnight. Turn them halfway through marinating. Remove from the beer bath and discard the beer.

3. Using a smoker or a domed charcoal grill, make sure there is no fire directly under the meat. If using a grill, place a small pile of charcoal briquets under one side of the grill and, once the coals are white, add a few moistened wood chips, and close the dome. Whatever type of smoker/grill you use, do not allow the internal temperature to exceed 225°F (110°C). Thus, add only a couple briquets and handful of wood chips at a time without allowing the fire to go out.

BOURBON BARBECUE SAUCE

4 cups (960 ml) tomato paste

8 cups (1.9 L) hot water

1 whole lemon (squeeze in the juice and include the cut-up pieces)

1 cup (240 ml) apple cider vinegar

2 tablespoons yellow mustard

1 cup (220 g) packed dark brown sugar

2 tablespoons salt

2 tablespoons onion powder

1 tablespoon black pepper

4 tablespoons dark chili powder

12 ounces (360 ml) bourbon

4. Place the well-seasoned ribs on the smoker rack, bone side down. Once the ribs become a nice brown hue—this will take several hours; you do not have to flip them—remove them from the smoker/grill, wrap them in aluminum foil, and return them to the smoker/grill. Continue cooking for about 2 hours longer. (Length of time depends on the size of the ribs.) When you can easily push your finger through the thickest part of the ribs, they are ready.

5. **Meanwhile, make the bourbon barbecue sauce:** In a large bowl, combine all the sauce ingredients and mix well.

6. Open the foil and brush the ribs with the bourbon BBQ sauce. Allow them to heat on the smoker/grill until the sauce bubbles, 30 to 45 minutes longer. Let rest for 10 minutes, then separate the bones and enjoy.

NOTE: *Getting the fire just right is key. At my restaurant, I use a combination of hickory and cherry wood to smoke. However, there are several other types—e.g., apple, pecan, oak, and mesquite—that reap great results. Because we smoke such large quantities, we use a large commercial Ole Hickory smoker, but any type will suffice, as long as you use the displaced smoking method.*

BREWSERTS
& BREAD

BEER SUMMIT

During the summer of 2009, I was determined to make the beer cut for President Obama's "beer summit." I knew our Sugar Hill Golden Ale would not only be the perfect flavor for diffusing tensions, but also reflect cultural roots that resonated with everyone.

My excitement bubbled over as I embarked on a quest to deliver the brews to Professor Henry Louis Gates Jr. on Martha's Vineyard for this momentous occasion. I loaded my car with several cases and set out on the journey with the aroma of beer filling the air. The road ahead led me through vibrant cityscapes and scenic routes, each mile of anticipation bringing me closer to my destination. I arrived at the Woods Hole Terminal to catch the ferry, drove my car with my precious cargo onto it, and set sail with a sip.

When I reached the island, I rented a bike to personally deliver the beer to Professor Skip Gates. Riding through the charming streets, I felt a sense of accomplishment and pride. Arriving at his home, I could envision the beer becoming a centerpiece during this historic "beer summit" at the White House. I knew it was a long shot, but I hoped the beer would not only delight the taste buds, but also be a symbol of unity during an important moment in history.

Well, needless to say, after all that, the "beer summit" featured Bud Light, Blue Moon and Red Stripe!

BREWNANA PUDDING

Step right into the heart of Aunt Bettie's kitchen with this delightful twist on a classic family reunion favorite: banana pudding. The rich tapestry of flavors in this recipe pays homage to traditional banana pudding while adding a new layer with the infusion of wheat beer.

SERVES 6

---

2 cups (480 ml) almond or oat milk

½ teaspoon vanilla extract

1 box (4.6 ounces, or 130 g) vanilla instant pudding mix

1 tablespoon unsalted butter

6 medium bananas, sliced

2 tablespoons sugar

2 ounces (60 ml) Renaissance Wit (or a similar beer)

1 box (11 ounces, or 312 g) vanilla wafer cookies (such as Nilla Wafers)

1. In a medium bowl, whisk together the milk and vanilla. Add the pudding mix and whisk until thickened.

2. In a large skillet, melt the butter over medium heat. Add the bananas and sugar and cook, stirring occasionally, until the bananas are golden brown and caramelized on both sides, making sure not to burn them.

3. Pour the beer over the bananas and let cook for 1 minute, or until most of the beer has evaporated.

4. In an 8 x 8-inch (20 x 20 cm) glass baking dish, add one-third of the pudding, followed by one-third of the bananas, and then one-third of the vanilla wafers in a single layer. Repeat this step two more times with the remaining pudding, bananas, and wafers. Cover and refrigerate for at least 1 hour before serving.

BREWSY PEACH COBBLER

The marriage of sweet, juicy peaches and crisp notes of Lenox Lager gives warmth to this cobbler, with layers of cinnamon and ginger adding spice. It's sure to become a cherished addition to your culinary repertoire.

SERVES 6 TO 8

3 ounces (90 ml) Lenox Lager (or a similar beer)

6 ripe peaches, pitted and sliced

2 cups (440 g) packed brown sugar, divided

1 teaspoon ground cinnamon

1 tablespoon fresh lemon juice

1 tablespoon cornstarch

1½ cups (190 g) all-purpose flour

1½ tablespoons baking powder

1 cup (240 ml) milk

Vanilla ice cream, for serving (optional)

1. Preheat the oven to 350°F (175°C).

2. In a large bowl, combine the beer, peach slices, 1 cup (220 g) of the brown sugar, the cinnamon, lemon juice, and cornstarch. Mix thoroughly, then pour into a 9 x 13-inch (23 x 33 cm) baking dish.

3. Bake for 20 minutes, or until lightly browned, thick, and syrupy.

4. Meanwhile, combine the flour, remaining 1 cup (220 g) brown sugar, and baking powder in a large bowl. Add the milk and whisk until thoroughly combined.

5. Spread the batter over the peaches. Bake for 30 minutes, or until golden brown.

6. If using, serve with a scoop of ice cream on top of each portion.

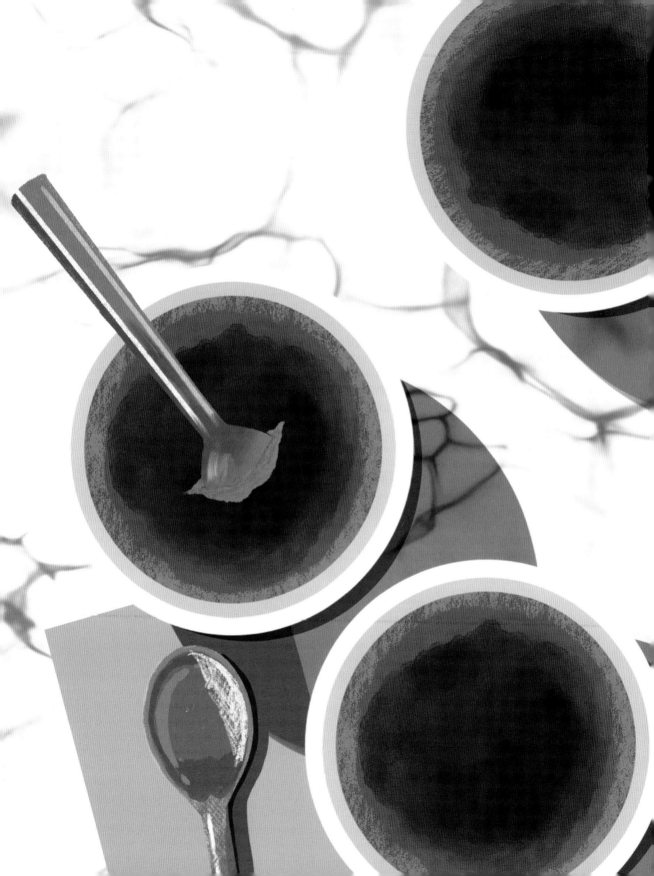

COFFEE STOUT CRÈME BREWLÉE

This smooth, soulful custard, kissed with chocolate and coffee notes and crowned with a perfectly caramelized crust, is hearty and flavorful, and makes a perfectly satisfying, decadent treat.

MAKES 6 BRÛLÉES

---

4 cups (1 quart, or 1 L) heavy cream

1 vanilla bean, split and seeds scraped

6 egg yolks

1 cup (200 g) sugar, divided

2 ounces (60 ml) Queen Stout (or a similar beer)

8 cups (2 quarts, or 2 L) hot water

1. Preheat the oven to 325°F (165°C).

2. In a medium heavy saucepan, bring the heavy cream, vanilla bean and seeds to a slight boil over medium-high heat, then whisk. Remove from the heat, cover, and let sit for 15 minutes.

3. In a medium bowl, whisk together the egg yolks, ½ cup (100 g) of the sugar, and the beer.

4. Slowly pour the cream-vanilla mixture into the bowl with the yolks while constantly whisking.

5. Fill six 8-ounce (237 ml) ramekins with the custard mixture. Place the ramekins in a large roasting pan, then add the hot water halfway up the sides of the ramekins.

6. Carefully transfer the pan to the oven and bake until the brûlées are set in the center, about 1 hour. Slowly and carefully remove the ramekins from the water. Let cool completely, then refrigerate, covered, overnight.

7. When ready to serve, preheat the broiler of the oven. Sprinkle each brûlée with 1 teaspoon of the remaining sugar and broil until the sugar caramelizes but does not burn. Let cool a bit before serving.

PEANUT BEERITTLE

Ready, set, go . . . right back to a nostalgic childhood favorite with a grown-up twist. Imagine the satisfying crunch of peanuts enveloped in a delicate caramelized coating, infused with our Queen Stout brew. Whether you're reminiscing about carefree days or simply seeking a delightful indulgence with a sophisticated edge, this beerittle is sure to satisfy your cravings

SERVES 12

Baking spray

2 cups (400 g) sugar

1 cup (240 ml) light corn syrup

4 ounces (120 ml) Queen Stout (or a similar beer)

½ teaspoon salt

3 cups (450 g) raw whole peanuts

2 teaspoons baking soda

4 teaspoons unsalted butter

1. Grease two baking sheets with baking spray.

2. In a medium saucepan, combine the sugar, corn syrup, beer, 1 cup (240 ml) of water, and salt and bring to a boil over medium-high heat. Stir in the peanuts.

3. Insert a candy thermometer into the mixture, reduce the heat to medium-low and let simmer until the temperature reaches 300°F (150°C) and is thick and golden brown.

4. Remove the pan from the heat, add the baking soda and butter, and mix thoroughly with a wooden spoon until it thickens.

5. Pour the mixture onto the prepared baking sheets and spread it as thinly as possible with a spatula.

6. Let cool completely, then break into pieces. Store in an airtight container.

STOUT BEEROWNIES

Journey into the realm of decadence with Chef Malik's extraordinary stout brownies. In this twist on a personal favorite, he has taken the humble brownie to new heights, uniting the deep, chocolate flavors of stout with the richness of cocoa powder.

SERVES 8 TO 10

½ cup (50 g) unsweetened cocoa powder

½ cup (1 stick, or 115 g) butter, melted

¼ cup (60 ml) Queen Stout Brewduction (page 160)

1 large egg

1 cup (200 g) sugar

1½ cups (190 g) all-purpose flour

Pinch of salt

Nonstick cooking spray

1. Preheat the oven to 350°F (175°C).

2. In a large bowl, combine the cocoa powder, melted butter, and brewduction and mix well. Stir in the egg.

3. In a medium bowl, combine the sugar, flour, and salt and mix well.

4. Stir the dry ingredients into the wet ingredients until combined.

5. Pour the batter into a 9 x 9-inch (23 x 23 cm) glass baking dish greased with cooking spray.

6. Bake for 25 minutes, or until the brownies are slightly firm to the touch. Let cool completely in the pan before slicing.

GRANDMA RUBELLE'S RICE PUDDING

Growing up, Grandma Rubelle's kitchen was like a magic show! There was always something surprising and delicious unfolding right before our eyes and noses. When it came to dessert, hers were the most heartwarming. This rice pudding made with Queen Stout is a testament to her adventurous spirit and love for reinventing classic recipes. By blending the creamy comfort of rice pudding with the complex notes of stout, this take on her homegrown recipe is sure to lift your spirits and taste buds and become a new favorite.

SERVES 4

½ cup (100 g) short-grain white rice

1½ cups (360 ml) scalded milk

2 ounces (60 ml) Queen Stout (or a similar beer)

2 egg yolks, beaten

½ cup (120 ml) heavy cream

2 tablespoons brown sugar

1 tablespoon vanilla extract

Ground cinnamon, for topping

1. In a large saucepan, combine the rice, scalded milk, and beer and cook over medium-high heat until bubbles start to form. Reduce the heat to low and cook for 10 minutes.

2. Meanwhile, combine the egg yolks, cream, sugar, and vanilla in a medium bowl and mix well. Slowly add this mixture to the pot with the rice, stirring constantly to combine. Cook for 45 minutes over low heat, stirring constantly, or until thick and creamy.

3. Preheat the broiler of the oven. Transfer the rice pudding to an 8 x 8-inch (20 x 20 cm) baking dish. Broil until browned on top, about 1 to 2 minutes. Let cool, then sprinkle with cinnamon.

4. Serve warm or chilled.

STOUT-GLAZED CINNAMON APPLES

Apple season is a favorite time of the year! This soul-warming and cherished recipe is one of my mother's favorites—a fantastic blend of apple sweetness with a warm embrace of cinnamon, brown sugar, and a splash of Queen Stout. The result is a jam session for the palate and a delightful treat for any time of the year.

SERVES 6 TO 8

4 large apples, peeled, cored, and sliced

1 tablespoon fresh lemon juice

8 ounces (240 ml) Queen Stout (or a similar beer)

½ cup (110 g) packed brown sugar

1 teaspoon ground cinnamon, plus more for garnishing

2 tablespoons unsalted butter

Pinch of salt

Vanilla ice cream, for serving (optional)

Whipped cream, for topping (optional)

1. In a large bowl, toss the sliced apples with the lemon juice to prevent browning.

2. In a medium saucepan over medium heat, combine the beer, brown sugar, cinnamon, butter, and salt and stir until the sugar dissolves and the mixture is simmering, 3 to 5 minutes.

3. Pour the beer glaze over the sliced apples, then add the mixture with the apples and glaze back into the saucepan over medium heat. Let the mixture simmer, stirring occasionally, until the apples are tender and the glaze thickens to a syrupy consistency, 10 to 12 minutes.

4. Spoon the warm, beer-infused cinnamon apples over vanilla ice cream (if using) or enjoy them on their own.

5. Sprinkle with cinnamon and top with whipped cream (if using).

BLACKBEERRY SORBET

Indulge in the delightful union of sweet blackberries and the refreshing Renaissance Wit with this homemade sorbet, perfect for cooling off on warm summer days or as a delightful palate cleanser between courses.

SERVES 6

---

4 cups (560 g) fresh blackberries, plus more for garnishing (optional)

1 cup (200 g) sugar

6 ounces (180 ml) Renaissance Wit (or a similar beer)

2 tablespoons fresh lemon juice

Grated zest of 1 lemon

Pinch of salt

Ice cream cones, for serving (optional)

Sprigs fresh mint, for garnishing (optional)

1. Rinse the blackberries thoroughly under cold water and pat them dry.

2. Add the blackberries to a blender or food processor and blend until smooth. Strain the puree through a fine-mesh strainer to remove the seeds, pressing gently to extract as much juice as possible.

3. In a small saucepan, combine the sugar with 1 cup (240 ml) of water over medium heat. Stir until the sugar is completely dissolved, creating a simple syrup. Remove from the heat and let cool to room temperature.

4. In a large bowl, combine the blackberry puree, cooled simple syrup, beer, lemon juice and zest, and salt and stir until all ingredients are well incorporated. Cover the bowl with plastic wrap and refrigerate for at least 2 hours, or until thoroughly chilled.

5. Pour the chilled mixture into an ice cream maker and churn according to the manufacturer's instructions. Churning time may vary but typically it takes 20 to 25 minutes, or until the sorbet reaches a thick, slushy consistency. Transfer the churned sorbet into a freezer-safe container.

6. Cover the container with a lid or plastic wrap and freeze for 4 to 6 hours, or until the sorbet is firm.

7. Once firm, scoop the sorbet into bowls or cones. Garnish with fresh blackberries (if using) and/or a sprig of mint (if using). Serve immediately.

CORN BEEREAD

Inhale the aroma of freshly baked corn bread as it wafts through the house, its golden crust glistening with promise and the hoppy flavors of IPA adding depth to every crumb.

SERVES 6 TO 8

Nonstick cooking spray

2 cups (250 g) all-purpose flour

1 cup (135 g) self-rising cornmeal

1 teaspoon baking powder

1 teaspoon salt

1 tablespoon honey

12 ounces (360 ml) 125th Street IPA (or a similar beer)

2 tablespoons melted butter

1. Preheat the oven to 350°F (175°C). Lightly grease a 9-inch (23 cm) loaf pan with cooking spray.

2. In a medium bowl, whisk together the flour, cornmeal, baking powder, and salt.

3. In a measuring cup, whisk together the honey and beer. Pour the beer-honey mixture into the dry ingredients and mix until just combined.

4. Pour the batter into the prepared loaf pan and drizzle with the melted butter.

5. Bake for 45 to 55 minutes, until a toothpick inserted in the center comes out clean and the bread is golden brown.

6. Let cool for 5 minutes in the pan before turning out onto a cooling rack. Serve warm.

WHOLE WHEAT BEEREAD

I love whole wheat bread, but there's nothing like hopping it up sometimes. This recipe combines whole wheat flour's nutty flavor with a beer buzz! Filling and delicious, it's perfect for sandwiches, toasted with butter, or for sopping up homemade gravy.

SERVES 12 TO 16

Nonstick cooking spray

3 cups (375 g) whole wheat flour

1 cup (125 g) all-purpose flour

⅓ teaspoon baking powder

1 teaspoon salt

12 ounces (360 ml) cold Renaissance Wit (or a similar beer)

3 tablespoons honey or maple syrup

¼ cup (½ stick, or 55 g) butter, melted, for coating

1. Preheat the oven to 375°F (190°C). Grease a loaf pan with cooking spray.

2. In a large bowl, combine the flours, baking powder, and salt and blend well.

3. In a measuring cup, whisk together the beer and honey. Add the mixture to the flour blend and stir with a wooden spoon until the flour is just incorporated; it will be a thick dough. Knead five times, then transfer to the prepared loaf pan.

4. Evenly brush the melted butter across the top of the dough.

5. Bake for 45 minutes, or until the internal temperature when tested with a thermometer is 190°F (88°C). Let cool in the pan for 10 minutes before transferring to a wire rack to cool completely. Slice and enjoy.

6. Store in a resealable plastic bag in the refrigerator for up to 2 weeks or on the counter for up to 1 week.

HOE-HOP CAKES

Hoecakes are timeless cornmeal perfection, sizzling in a cast-iron skillet, with their crisp edges and soft, pillowy centers. This iconic Southern staple has humble origins, cooked for family and community dinners, where hearty meals were shared and memories were made. Dip a hoecake into honey or some hot pinto beans topped with chopped onion (my favorite!), or enjoy as a side for fish and grits.

MAKES 8 CAKES

½ cup (90 g) yellow cornmeal

½ cup (65 g) all-purpose flour

1 teaspoon baking powder

1 teaspoon sugar

1½ teaspoons salt

3 tablespoons unsalted butter, melted

4 ounces (120 ml) Lenox Lager (or a similar beer)

½ cup (120 ml) slightly boiling water

2 large eggs

¼ cup (35 g) frozen corn kernels, thawed

Neutral oil, for frying

1. In a medium bowl, whisk together the cornmeal, flour, baking powder, sugar, and salt.

2. In a small bowl, whisk together the melted butter and beer. Add the wet ingredients to the dry ingredients and stir until the batter is well combined but not too smooth; a few lumps are good.

3. Add the slightly boiling water to the bowl, followed by the eggs, one at a time, continually stirring so as not to scramble the eggs but incorporate them. (If the dough is very thick, add another egg.) Fold in the corn kernels and mix well.

4. In a large cast-iron skillet, heat 1 inch (2.5 cm) of oil over medium-high heat. Once hot, working in batches, add 2 tablespoons of the batter for each cake and cook until bubbles form on top. Flip over and cook until the bottom is golden, 2 to 3 minutes per side. Serve hot.

CORN BEEREAD STUFFING

This corn-bread stuffing brings lots of Southern comfort to the holidays. Our recipe pays homage to generations of family cooks who have perfected the art of combining simple ingredients to create extraordinary flavors. By incorporating beer into the mix, we have added another layer of richness to each spoonful of this savory stuffing. You'll taste the warmth of tradition and the joy of gathering with loved ones in laughter-filled kitchens of generations past, where family recipes have been passed down with love and care. Grab your apron and create memories that will last a lifetime.

SERVES 6 TO 8

1 batch corn bread

½ cup (1 stick, or 115 g) unsalted butter

1 large onion, finely chopped

3 ribs celery, finely chopped

3 cloves garlic, minced

8 ounces (240 ml) 125th Street IPA (or a similar beer)

1 teaspoon dried thyme

1 teaspoon dried sage

Salt and black pepper

2 cups (480 ml) chicken or vegetable broth

2 large eggs

Finely chopped fresh parsley, for garnishing

1. Preheat the oven to 375°F (190°C). Grease a 9 x 13-inch (23 x 33 cm) baking dish with cooking spray.

2. In a large bowl, crumble the corn bread into tiny pieces.

3. In a large skillet, melt the butter over medium heat. Add the onion, celery, and garlic and cook and stir until the onion is softened and translucent, 5 to 7 minutes.

4. Add the beer to the saucepan and let simmer for 2 to 3 minutes, until the beer has reduced by half. Add the thyme and sage, season with salt and pepper, and stir well.

5. Pour the beer-vegetable mixture over the crumbled corn bread and toss to combine.

6. In a medium bowl, whisk together the broth and eggs. Pour the mixture over corn bread and blend well.

7. Pour the stuffing mixture into the prepared baking dish and evenly spread it.

8. Bake for 40 to 45 minutes, until the top is crispy and golden brown.

9. Before serving, garnish with fresh parsley.

QUEEN STOUT CAKE

My niece Emma baked this cake for my mother's eighty-fourth birthday. The beer has bold, deep coffee and chocolate character that complements the sweet malted barley. Topped with a layer of stout cream frosting, it's truly bittersweet!

SERVES 8 TO 10

CAKE

10 tablespoons (142 g) butter, melted, plus more for greasing

8 ounces (240 ml) Queen Stout (or a similar beer)

¾ cup (85 g) cocoa powder

1 cup (225 g) granulated sugar

1⅓ cups (225 g) dark brown sugar

¾ cup (170 g) sour cream

2 large eggs, at room temperature

1 tablespoon vanilla extract

2 cups (284 g) all-purpose flour

1½ teaspoons baking soda

1 teaspoon salt

1. **To make the cake:** Preheat the oven to 350°F (175°C). Butter and line a 9-inch (23 cm) springform pan with parchment paper and set aside.

2. Using either a stand mixer or a hand mixer and a large bowl, beat the beer, melted butter, cocoa powder, granulated sugar, and brown sugar on medium-low speed for 3 minutes, or until the sugars have dissolved and the mixture has lightened in color and become fluffier in texture.

3. Add the sour cream and continue to beat on medium-low speed for 30 seconds, or until incorporated. Add the eggs and vanilla and continue to beat on medium-low until all is incorporated, about 2 minutes longer.

4. In a medium bowl, whisk together the flour, baking soda, and salt. Slowly add the flour mixture into the wet mixture and beat on medium-low until combined, about 2 minutes. Pour the batter into the prepared pan.

5. Bake for 45 to 60 minutes, until a toothpick or skewer inserted in the center of the cake comes out clean. Let the cake cool completely in the pan.

(continued)

FROSTING

½ cup (1 stick) unsalted butter, at room temperature

1 pound (454 g) confectioners' sugar, sifted

2 squares unsweetened dark chocolate, melted and cooled slightly

¼ cup (60 ml) Queen Stout (or a similar beer)

1 tablespoon vanilla extract

6. **While the cake cools, make the frosting:** Add the butter to a large bowl and mix with an electric mixer on medium-high until light and fluffy, about 3 minutes.

7. Add the confectioners' sugar, chocolate, beer, and vanilla to the bowl and continue to beat on medium speed until all is incorporated and the frosting is light and fluffy, about 3 minutes longer.

8. Once the cake is completely cooled, remove it from the pan. Frost the entire cake with the frosting, then slice and serve it. Store any leftovers in an airtight container in the refrigerator for up to 1 week.

NOTE: *Use the stout cream frosting to enhance your favorite cakes and cupcakes.*

SAUCES, RUBS & BEERINADES

QUEEN STOUT BREWDUCTION

This versatile condiment can be drizzled over meats and roasted vegetables or used as a dipping sauce for crusty bread, adding depth and complexity to your culinary creations.

12 ounces (360 ml) Queen Stout (or a similar beer)

1 tablespoon black pepper

1 piece (1 inch, or 2.5 cm) cinnamon stick

1 bay leaf

1. In a medium pot, combine all the ingredients and cook over medium heat until the liquid reduces by one-third, 10 to 12 minutes.

2. Remove from the heat and let cool. Remove and discard the cinnamon stick and bay leaf.

3. Store in an airtight container in the refrigerator for up to 2 weeks.

SPICY BREWMOULADE

This brewmoulade is a versatile companion that adds a spicy twist to your favorite dishes. Whether you're hosting a barbecue or looking to spice up your everyday meals, this is just the ingredient you need!

2 ounces (60 ml) Renaissance Wit (or a similar beer)

1 cup (240 ml) mayonnaise

½ cup (120 g) sweet pickle relish

Zest and juice of 1 lemon

2 tablespoons Dijon mustard

½ teaspoon cayenne pepper

2 tablespoons finely chopped scallion

¼ cup (10 g) finely chopped fresh cilantro

Salt and black pepper

1. In a medium bowl, whisk together the beer, mayonnaise, relish, lemon zest and juice, Dijon mustard, and cayenne until well blended.

2. Add the chopped scallion and cilantro to the mixture, stirring to incorporate. Season with salt and pepper.

3. Cover and let chill in the refrigerator for at least 30 minutes to let the flavors meld.

4. Store any unused brewmoulade in an airtight container in the refrigerator for up to 3 days.

ROSEMARY RUB

Rosemary is the herb that keeps on giving through all the seasons. I literally use rosemary for everything: body, spirit, and food! Use this rub for vegetables, chicken, lamb, turkey, and fish.

3 tablespoons finely chopped fresh rosemary

2 teaspoons Himalayan salt

1 tablespoon black pepper

½ tablespoon paprika

½ teaspoon ground cumin

½ teaspoon hops flower powder

¼ teaspoon smoked cayenne pepper

1 teaspoon dried cilantro

1 teaspoon mustard powder

1 teaspoon onion powder

1. Add all the ingredients to a blender and process until a powder.

2. Store in a sealed bottle or jar in the refrigerator for up to 2 weeks or in the freezer for up to 1 month.

BROWN SUGAR RUB

We come from a long line of BBQ pitmasters. This rub is ideal for poultry, pork, and beef. Just rub it into meats or ribs and refrigerate for 6 to 8 hours, or overnight, then grill the meat, or slow-cook it in a smoker to maximize the flavors of this rub.

½ cup (110 g) packed dark brown sugar

2 tablespoons salt

¼ cup (24 g) black pepper

1 tablespoon onion powder

1 tablespoon ground cumin

2 tablespoons garlic powder

2 teaspoons cayenne pepper

½ teaspoon hops flower powder

1. In a medium bowl, combine all the ingredients.

BAR-BEER-QUE SAUCE

This jaw-dropping creation with its savory and sweet ingredients promises to heighten your barbecue experience. With each brushstroke, your meats will be enveloped in a luscious glaze with a hint of beer.

6 ounces (180 ml) 125th Street IPA (or a similar beer)

2 cloves garlic, minced

2 cups (480 ml) ketchup

1 tablespoon hot sauce

½ cup (120 ml) soy sauce or Worcestershire sauce

1 teaspoon mustard powder

¼ cup (55 g) packed brown sugar

4 ounces (120 ml) whiskey

3 teaspoons smoked chili powder

1 teaspoon cayenne pepper

1 teaspoon ground cumin

½ teaspoon paprika

1. Combine all the ingredients in a large saucepan over medium-high heat. Bring to a boil, reduce the heat to low, and let simmer for 1 hour, or until thick and the flavors have melded and developed.

2. Store in an airtight container in the refrigerator for up to 1 month.

BERRY BEERNAIGRETTE

Whether drizzled over crisp summer salads or used as a marinade for grilled meats, this beernaigrette promises a vibrant burst of flavor.

2 cups (250 g) fresh or frozen (thawed) raspberries

½ cup (120 ml) apple cider vinegar

4 ounces (120 ml) Renaissance Wit (or a similar beer)

1 tablespoon honey

1 teaspoon fresh lemon juice

1. Add all the ingredients to a blender and process for 2 minutes, or until smooth. Pour through a fine-mesh strainer into a bottle with a lid. Store in an airtight container in the refrigerator for up to 1 week.

2. Shake well to blend before using.

CURRY SAUCE

There are so many variations of curry including Indian, Jamaican, and Thai, among others. I really enjoy the blend of spices in curry and how it marries with beer, especially in my stews. This saucy fusion of flavors promises to have your taste buds hoppin' around to distant lands, where aromatic spices mingle with the deep richness of beer.

2 tablespoons salted butter

2 medium white onions, chopped

1 clove garlic, chopped

6 ounces (180 ml) 125th Street IPA (or a similar beer)

2 bay leaves

4 tablespoons curry powder

½ teaspoon dried thyme

1 tablespoon salt

2 tablespoons tomato paste

2 tablespoons grated coconut

2 green apples, chopped

4 cups (1 quart, or 1 L) chicken or vegetable stock or water

1. In a large stockpot, melt the butter over medium heat. Add the onions and garlic and cook and stir for 3 minutes, or until they begin to soften.

2. Add the beer, bay leaves, curry powder, thyme, salt, tomato paste, coconut, apples, and stock to the pot and bring to a boil over medium-high heat. Reduce the heat to medium-low and let simmer for 1 hour, or until the flavors are well developed and the sauce has thickened.

3. Strain through a fine-mesh strainer and let cool. Store in an airtight container in the refrigerator for up to 1 month.

TIPSY TOMATILLO SAUCE

I like to dip my shrimp into this sauce or spread it over baked or grilled fish. For the past few years I've had a bumper crop of tomatillos from seeds I planted.

1 pound (454 g) tomatillos, papery outside peeled and cut in half

2 ounces (60 ml) Renaissance Wit (or a similar beer)

2 cloves garlic, chopped

¼ cup (30 g) chopped onion

½ tablespoon chopped seeded jalapeño

¼ cup (10 g) finely chopped fresh cilantro

½ cup (120 ml) olive oil

¼ cup (60 ml) fresh lime juice

1 tablespoon sugar

1. Preheat the broiler of the oven.

2. Place the tomatillo halves, cut sides up, on a baking sheet and broil for 5 minutes, or until charred in places and softened.

3. Add the tomatillos, beer, garlic, onion, jalapeño, cilantro, oil, lime juice, and sugar to a blender and process until smooth and creamy.

4. Store in an airtight container in the refrigerator for up to 1 week.

BEERINE

Brining with beer instead of water adds more flavor and moisture. This brine is a game changer for poultry. Brine chicken wings for 4 to 6 hours, drain, and cook them your favorite way.

1 cup (240 ml) boiling water

½ cup (110 g) packed brown sugar

3 tablespoons salt

36 ounces (1.1 L) 125th Street IPA (or a similar beer)

3 sprigs fresh rosemary

½ cup (55 g) chopped onion

4 cloves garlic, chopped

1 jalapeño pepper, chopped

2 tablespoons black pepper

1. In a large pot or Dutch oven, combine the boiling water, brown sugar, and salt and stir to dissolve the sugar. Let cool.

2. Once the sugar water is cool, add the beer, rosemary, onion, garlic, jalapeño, and black pepper.

BEEROWN SAUCE

This classic brown sauce, created by Chef K, is great when drizzled over a perfectly seared steak, smothering a mound of mashed potatoes, or paired with your favorite roasted vegetables.

3 tablespoons butter

3 shallots or scallions, finely chopped

6 ounces (180 ml) Sugar Hill Golden Ale (or a similar beer)

1 can (10.5 ounces, or 298 g) beef broth or consommé

1 teaspoon dried tarragon

Pinch of dried thyme

1 tablespoon cornstarch

2 tablespoons cold water

Salt and black pepper

1. In a large skillet, melt the butter over medium heat. Add the shallots and cook and stir for 5 minutes, or until softened and lightly caramelized. Gradually add the beer and broth. Increase the heat to medium-high and let come to a boil. Add the tarragon and thyme and season with salt and pepper. Reduce the heat to medium and let the liquid reduce by half, 7 to 10 minutes.

2. In a small bowl, whisk together the cornstarch and cold water. Add the mixture to the pan and let simmer for 2 minutes, or until thickened. Strain through a fine-mesh strainer and let cool.

3. Store in an airtight container in the refrigerator for up to 1 week.

CHIPOTLE PEACH SAUCE

This sauce has the perfect balance of sweet and heat. Drizzle it over grilled chicken or pork for a mouthwatering experience.

1 tablespoon olive oil

1 tablespoon chopped shallot

2 cups (310 g) pitted, peeled, and chopped peaches

12 ounces (360 ml) Summer Soul Ale (or a similar beer)

1 teaspoon sauce from chipotle peppers in adobo sauce

6 tablespoons chicken stock

1. In a large skillet, heat the oil over medium heat. Add the shallot and cook and stir until just tender. Add the peaches and beer and let simmer until reduced by half, about 30 minutes, stirring occasionally.

2. Stir in the adobo sauce and chicken stock and let simmer for 5 more minutes. Remove from the heat and let cool until lukewarm.

3. Transfer to a blender and process on high speed until smooth.

CHOCOLATE COFFEE STOUT BEERINADE

This marinade is great for beef or pork; just let the meat marinate in the refrigerator for a few hours, or overnight, for the flavors to infuse.

8 ounces (240 ml) Queen Stout (or a similar beer)

½ cup (70 g) chopped garlic, or to taste

2 tablespoons smoked paprika

2 tablespoons brown sugar

½ cup (120 ml) olive oil

1. In a large bowl, combine all the ingredients and mix well. Store in an airtight container in the refrigerator for up to 1 week prior to using.

2. To marinate beef or pork, combine the marinade and meat in a container or bowl, cover, and let marinate in the refrigerator for 1 to 24 hours. Remove from the marinade and cook as you wish.

SAGE THYME BEERINADE

Use this herby marinade for all meats, especially chicken and fish, as well as your veggies. Try it with broccoli, squash, and corn.

1 ounce (30 ml) Sugar Hill Golden Ale (or a similar beer)

¼ cup (60 ml) balsamic vinegar

1 tablespoon dried thyme

1 tablespoon dried sage

¼ cup (15 g) chopped scallion

1. In a large bowl, combine all the ingredients and mix well. Store in an airtight container in the refrigerator for up to 1 week prior to using.

2. To use as a marinade, combine the beerinade and your favorite chopped chicken or turkey in a bowl, cover and refrigerate for 2 to 24 hours. Remove from the marinade and cook as you wish. Discard the marinade.

JERKY TURKEY BEERINADE

We first tried this beerinade with a turkey we planned to deep-fry—our first one!—when visiting friends for Thanksgiving. We packed up a few six-packs of Renaissance Wit and drove to Lynchburg, Virginia, for the feast and fun.

½ cup (120 ml) lemon juice

4 ounces (120 ml) Renaissance Wit (or a similar beer)

½ cup (120 ml) liquid crab boil seasoning

½ cup (120 ml) olive oil

½ cup (1 stick, or 115 g) unsalted butter

2 tablespoons onion powder

2 tablespoons garlic powder

2 tablespoons Cajun seasoning

1 teaspoon Tabasco sauce

1 teaspoon cayenne pepper

1. Place all the ingredients in a large bowl and whisk to combine. Store in an airtight container in the refrigerator for up to 2 weeks prior to using.

2. Follow directions for your favorite injected deep-fried turkey.

RENAISSANCE WIT BEERNAIGRETTE

Whether tossed with crisp lettuce, roasted vegetables, or grilled meats, every drizzle of this beernaigrette is refreshing, tangy, citrusy, and fragrant.

½ cup (120 ml) light olive oil

⅓ cup (80 ml) Renaissance Wit (or a similar beer)

1 teaspoon kosher salt

½ teaspoon Dijon mustard

⅛ teaspoon ground coriander

1. In a small bowl, whisk together all the ingredients using a fork, or shake in a jar with a tight-fitting lid.

2. Store in airtight container in the refrigerator for up to 1 month.

SOUL FOOD PLAYLIST

I rallied the troops—friends, family, and fellow beer enthusiasts—to concoct the ultimate soul food playlist. And let me tell you, the results are EPIC! With everyone pitching in their favorite tunes, we've curated a masterpiece that's sure to elevate every culinary adventure in the kitchen. From rockin' anthems to chill vibes, this playlist is the secret ingredient to making every beer-infused dish a culinary sensation. Cheers to collaboration and the magic of music and brews coming together!

RAGTIME

"Pekin Rag" by Joe Jordan

"The Entertainer" by Scott Joplin

"Harlem Rag" by Tom Turpin

"Magnetic Rag" by Scott Joplin

"Heliotrope Bouquet" by Scott Joplin and Louis Chauvin

"The Pearls" by Jelly Roll Morton

"Doing the Sugar Heel" by Reginald R. Robinson

"Grace and Beauty" by James Scott

"Dill Pickles Rag" by Charles L. Johnson

"Echoes of Spring" by Willie "The Lion" Smith

BLUES

"Sweet Home Chicago" by Robert Johnson

"Call It Stormy Monday (But Tuesday Is Just as Bad)" by T-Bone Walker

"The Thrill Is Gone" by B.B. King

"Good Morning Little Schoolgirl" by Sonny Boy Williamson

"Born Under a Bad Sign" by Albert King

"Every Day I Have the Blues" by Memphis Slim

"Hoochie Coochie Man" by Muddy Waters

"Dust My Broom" by Elmore James

"Crossroads" by Cream

"I'd Rather Go Blind" by Etta James

JAZZ

"Take Five" by Dave Brubeck

"Feeling Good" by Nina Simone

"Summertime" by Ella Fitzgerald and Louis Armstrong

"So What" by Miles Davis

"Fly Me to the Moon" by Frank Sinatra

"My Favorite Things" by John Coltrane

"Georgia on My Mind" by Ray Charles

"Autumn Leaves" by Cannonball Adderley

"Blue Monk" by Thelonious Monk

"In a Sentimental Mood" by Duke Ellington and John Coltrane

R & B

"Freedom" by Jon Batiste

"I Love Music" by The O'Jays

"Saturday Night Fish Fry" by Pearl Bailey and Moms Mabley

"Respect" by Aretha Franklin

"Let's Stay Together" by Al Green

"I'll Take You There" by The Staple Singers

"What's Going On" by Marvin Gaye

"I Say a Little Prayer" by Aretha Franklin

"Stand by Me" by Ben E. King

"At Last" by Etta James

"I Heard It Through the Grapevine" by Gladys Knight & The Pips

"Don't Stop 'Til You Get Enough by Michael Jackson

HIP-HOP

"Empire State of Mind" by Jay-Z ft. Alicia Keys

"I Used to Love H.E.R." by Common

"Ms. Fat Booty" by Mos Def

"Juicy" by The Notorious B.I.G.

"Award Tour" by A Tribe Called Quest

"Rosa Parks" by OutKast

"The Food" by Common

"Electric Avenue" by Eddy Grant (for some old-school vibes)

"Can I Kick It?" by A Tribe Called Quest

"C.R.E.A.M." by Wu-Tang Clan

"Rapper's Delight" by The Sugarhill Gang

COUNTRY

"Beer Never Broke My Heart" by Luke Combs

"Beer Can't Fix" by Thomas Rhett ft. Jon Pardi

"Burgers and Fries" by Charlie Pride

"Beer Money" by Kip Moore

"Cornbread and Butterbeans" by The Carolina Chocolate Drops

"Drinkin' Problem" by Midland

"I Love This Bar" by Toby Keith

"Texas Hold 'Em" by Beyoncé

"Buy Me a Boat" by Chris Janson

"Beer in Mexico" by Kenny Chesney

"Friends in Low Places" by Garth Brooks

"Beers Ago" by Toby Keith

"Drunk on a Plane" by Dierks Bentley

BLUEGRASS

"I'd Rather Be" by Ebony Hillbillies

"Wagon Wheel" by Old Crow Medicine Show

"Man of Constant Sorrow" by Soggy Bottom Boys

"Rocky Top" by Osborne Brothers

"The Devil Went Down to Georgia" by The Charlie Daniels Band

"Roll in My Sweet Baby's Arms" by Flatt and Scruggs

"Blue Moon of Kentucky" by Bill Monroe

"I Am a Man of Constant Sorrow" by The Stanley Brothers

"Foggy Mountain Breakdown" by Flatt and Scruggs

"Nine Pound Hammer" by Del McCoury Band

"Uncle Pen" by Ricky Skaggs

ROCK

"Purple Haze" by Jimi Hendrix

"Bohemian Rhapsody" by Queen

"Hey Jude" by The Beatles

"Like a Rolling Stone" by Bob Dylan

"Hound Dog" by Big Mama Thornton

"I Still Haven't Found What I'm Looking For" by U2

"Born to Run" by Bruce Springsteen

"Hotel California" by Eagles

"Rock Steady" by Aretha Franklin

"Living for the City" by Stevie Wonder

"Clocks" by Coldplay

"Sussudio" by Phil Collins

INDEX

ACKNOWLEDGMENTS

This cookbook is a heartfelt tribute to the culinary artisans who have shaped our family's culinary legacy. Your unwavering dedication to crafting extraordinary meals at family celebrations has been a source of solace and nourishment, sustaining us through life's most challenging moments. With deep gratitude, I give thanks to the sacred traditions passed down through generations, cherished in both spoken word and the alchemy of food. Within these pages lies a heartfelt homage to the unsung heroes of home brewing, scattered across the Southern landscapes and woven into the tapestry of the African continent and beyond.

I extend heartfelt appreciation to my son, Khouri Beatty (Beer Chef; Chef K), whose innovative insights and contributions have infused this journey with boundless creativity. To my mother, Rachel Mae, whose kitchen served as the canvas for countless culinary experiments. To my father, Carl Beatty, whose culinary ingenuity birthed the unforgettable Salsibeery Steak dish. To my beloved siblings—Ayanna, Carl, Chris, Pernell, and Beverly—your steadfast support has been my guiding light.

To the guardians of our family's culinary traditions—Grandma Onie from the Crossroads of Wilmington, North Carolina, Grandma Ruby in Greensboro, North Carolina, and Grandma Mallen from Chicago—your wisdom and recipes continue to nourish our souls. I am deeply indebted to my aunts and uncles, whose culinary delights have filled our gatherings with joyous memories. Special gratitude to Linda Miller, a dear family friend whose culinary wisdom and boundless generosity have enriched this journey.

My gratitude and thanks to those who contributed recipes to this book: Chef Ed Wiley III, co-owner of The Prime Smokehouse in Rocky Mount, North Carolina (primesmokehouse.com); Chef Malik Williams, who specializes in Southern seed-to-table cuisine (@chefyoungboul); and Alexis Austin, a very talented mixologist at Chez Messy in Harlem, NYC (@chezmessy).

To my editor, Erin Canning, and everyone at Rock Point and The Quarto Group, thank-you for shepherding this labor of love to fruition. And to the luminaries Leah Chase and Verta Mae, your vibrant histories have ignited a fire within me, fueling my passion for cooking.

A heartfelt thanks to the vibrant community of Harlem, whose spirit has sustained me through the peaks and valleys of this endeavor. To the myriad restaurants and chefs along the I-95 corridor and beyond, your commitment to preserving the rich tapestry of Southern cooking rooted in the African diaspora has been a wellspring of inspiration.

To my friends in Richmond, Virginia, and throughout North Carolina, your culinary prowess has enriched this journey beyond measure.

Gratitude to the Greater Harlem Chamber of Commerce, Harlem Week, Harlem Business Alliance, NYC Brewers Guild, Brewers Association, OIC Rocky Mount, NB2A, Harlem Beer Distributing, Niche Brands, and all who have supported and collaborated with us.

Finally, immense appreciation to the Studio Museum, Apollo Theater, Jazz at Lincoln Center, the Jazz Foundation, and the Jazz Museum for providing the soulful soundtrack that continues to inspire and elevate our craft. Indeed, it takes a village to raise a beer!

ABOUT THE AUTHOR AND HARLEM BREWING COMPANY

Step into the extraordinary world of **CELESTE BEATTY**, a visionary and pioneer, shattering glass ceilings as the first Black woman to helm a brewery in the United States. Her journey is a tapestry of resilience, creativity, and community empowerment.

From her humble beginnings in the nonprofit sector, serving the marginalized and nurturing thearts, to comanaging the iconic Ben & Jerry's partner shop in the vibrant heart of Harlem, Celeste's path was destined for greatness. Yet, it was a fateful encounter with a home-brewing kit that ignited her passion for crafting exquisite beer. As she honed her skills, hosting intimate home-brewing classes and perfecting her craft, Celeste's dream blossomed into the renowned Harlem Brewing Company in 2000.

Under her stewardship, Harlem Brewing Company soared to new heights, capturing the hearts and palates of beer aficionados worldwide. From winning the prestigious People's Champ Award for Best Brews NYC to earning accolades at the esteemed Bacon and Beer Classic at Citi Field, Celeste's brews are hailed as works of art. But her impact extends far beyond accolades and acclaim. Celeste's brews transcend borders, captivating audiences in the United Kingdom and Japan with their exceptional quality and distinctive flavor profiles.

Her commitment to community is unwavering, as seen through partnerships with esteemed cultural institutions and charitable organizations, including the Dance Theater of Harlem, Jazz at Lincoln Center, and the Museum of African American History and Culture. As a founding board member of the National Black Brewers Association, Celeste continues to break barriers, championing diversity and inclusion in the brewing industry. Celeste's journey is a testament to the power of passion, perseverance, and the indomitable spirit of a true trailblazer.

Through her craft, she has not only crafted exceptional beer but also forged connections, fostered change, and inspired generations to come. This is more than a story of brewing; it's a tale of triumph, transformation, and the enduring legacy of a visionary.

HARLEM BREWING COMPANY is a pioneering craft brewery founded by Celeste Beatty in 2000. Inspired by the vibrant culture of Harlem, Celeste embarked on a mission to create flavorful and distinctive beers that reflect the spirit of the community. Breaking barriers as the first African American woman to launch a commercially distributed beer, Harlem Brewing Company has become a beacon of innovation and inclusion in the craft beer industry.

From their flagship Harlem "Sugar Hill" Golden Ale to their award-winning Harlem Renaissance Wit and Harlem 125th Street IPA, each brew tells a story of tradition, creativity, and pride. With a commitment to "Brewing It Forward," Harlem Brewing Company continues to push boundaries, celebrate diversity, and share the taste of Harlem with the world.

In 2018, Harlem Brewing Company expanded their brewing empire with the establishment of Harlem Brew South in Rocky Mount, North Carolina, bringing their distinct flavors to new audiences.

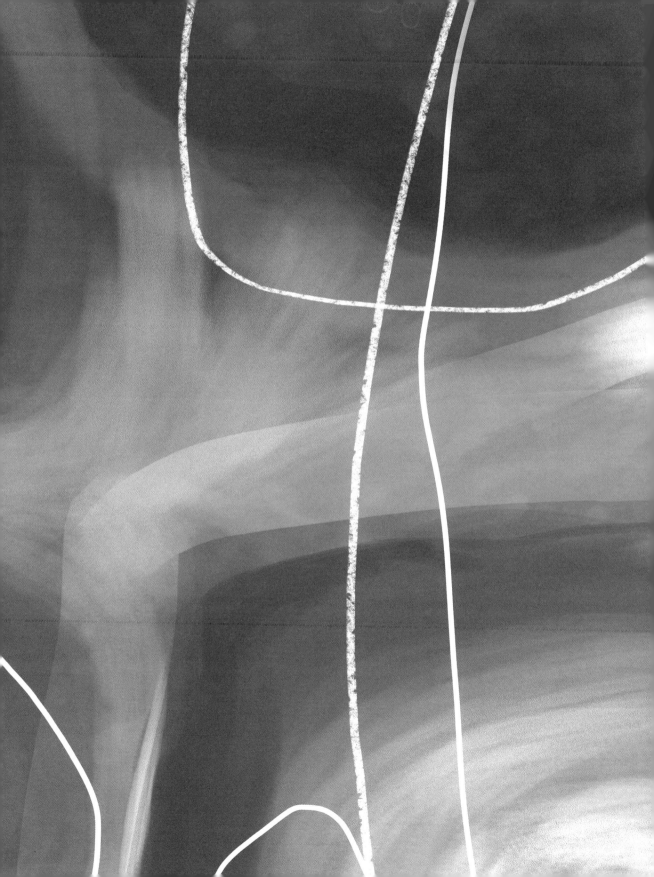